PACIFIC GROVE GUIDE BOOK

PACIFIC GROVE AT YOUR FEET

WALKS, HIKES & RAMBLES IN BUTTERFLY TOWN, USA

JOYCE KRIEG

ILLUSTRATIONS BY JUDY OBBINK

Pacific Grove Books
Pacific Grove, California

Pacific Grove at Your Feet, Walks, Hikes & Rambles in Butterfly Town U.S.A.—by Joyce Krieg
© 2020 Text, Joyce Krieg
FIRST EDITION January 2020   ISBN 978-1-943887-07-1

Every effort has been made to ensure that this book contains accurate and current information. The author and Pacific Grove Books bear no responsibility for changes in trail conditions, operating hours, and rules and regulations that may have occurred since the writing and research of this book in the spring and summer of 2019. The author and Pacific Grove Books shall not be liable for any loss or damage suffered by any readers as a result of any information contained herein.

PACIFIC GROVE BOOKS
An imprint of
Park Place Publications
Pacific Grove, CA
pacificgrovebooks.com

PACIFIC GROVE BOOKS
Pacific Grove, California

PACIFIC GROVE BOOKS

(see last page of this book for 2021 PG BOOK new releases)

Life in Pacific Grove California: Personal Stories by Residents and Visitors to Butterfly Town U.S.A. (Book 1)
Pacific Grove Writers • Keith Larson–illustrator – 2017
Trade: ISBN 978-1943887361 Case: ISBN 978-1943887545

Life in Pacific Grove California: Deeper Connections History, Stories, and Selected Essays (Book 2)
Pacific Grove Writers • Peter Mounteer-photographer – 2018
Trade: ISBN 978-1943887736, Case: ISBN 978-1943887828

A Quaint Town for a Killing
A P.G. Mystery by Jeffrey Whitmore
ISBN 978-1943887743 – 2018

Pacific Grove 1974: poems, drawings, woodcuts, prose
William Minor • ISBN 978-1943887729 – 2018

A donation is made to the Pacific Grove Library for every book sold.
Bringing Our Community Together – Through the Power of Story

The Hart Mansion,
Historic Downtown, Pacific Grove, CA

PACIFIC GROVE AT YOUR FEET
WALKS, HIKES & RAMBLES

City Map of Pacific Grove Walks   6-7
Introduction   9
Rules of the Road   12

#1. **Recreation Trail East:** This beautiful, easy walk along the bluffs overlooking Monterey Bay is suitable for all ages and abilities, taking you from a world-class destination to a popular local park. On the way, you'll follow an old railroad bed as you pass by a harbor seal birthing beach and a popular selfie site. **16**

#2. **Recreation Trail West:** Breathtaking vistas of Monterey Bay and its abundant wildlife await those who tread this popular path. Numerous turnouts on Ocean View Boulevard with stairways and access paths make it easy to join this walk anywhere, or to do it in stages. **28**

#3. **Asilomar Coast Trail:** offers an easy and relaxing walk on the rocky bluffs overlooking the Pacific Ocean with stunning vistas of crashing waves. Much of this hike is on boardwalk or packed, crushed granite, suitable for strollers and wheelchairs, although the complete trail does involve a short distance on loose, sandy soil. **38**

#4. **The Beach at Low Tide:** The low-tide walk is a glorious adventure right on the damp sand, taking you along two beautiful white sand beaches, best done in early fall..........**48**

#5. **Over the Boardwalk:** A mostly easy walk along the shoreline bluffs on a well-maintained boardwalk. A few yards over a relatively steep sand dune might elevate this walk from easy to moderate status......................................**58**

#6. **Asilomar Conference Grounds:** Explore the work of famed architect Julia Morgan in a beautiful natural setting, with optional side trips to a cottage with a Steinbeck connection and over the sand dunes............................**66**

#7. **Walkin' the Ghost Rails:** When wind or fog make a walk on the shoreline bluffs unpleasant, the old Southern Pacific railbed offers an appealing alternative, steeped in local lore and featuring two different golf courses.........................**80**

#8. **El Carmelo Cemetery and Point Pinos Lighthouse:** Lighthouses have traditionally served as symbols of safety and comfort, so it would seem a natural pairing– a walk through a cemetery and a visit to a lighthouse..**90**

#9. **The Monarch Butterfly Sanctuary:** In a book about walks in Butterfly Town U.S.A., of course we must include this easy stroll through the Monarch Butterfly Sanctuary. Best done between October and February, when our annual visitors are actually in town. **100**

#10. **George Washington Park:** An easy walk through a woodsy oasis in the middle of the city, with an intriguing backstory—that's George Washington Park. **106**

#11. **Lynn "Rip" Van Winkle Open Space:** Locals refer to this as "the dog park" and that says it all! **112**

#12. **Historic Downtown Pacific Grove:** A stroll through Pacific Grove's downtown district offers a panorama of history from prehistoric eras to the dawn of the digital age. **118**

#13. **Strolling with Steinbeck:** The Nobel Prize-winning author is usually associated with Salinas, but he has a strong connection with Pacific Grove, both as a resident and as a setting for his stories..**138**

#14. **Candy Cane Lane:** Our holiday bonus, a stroll through Pacific Grove's traditional Christmas-themed neighborhood, usually open the first Saturday in December and running through New Year's Eve. **148**

2021 NEW RELEASES – PACIFIC GROVE BOOKS................ 154

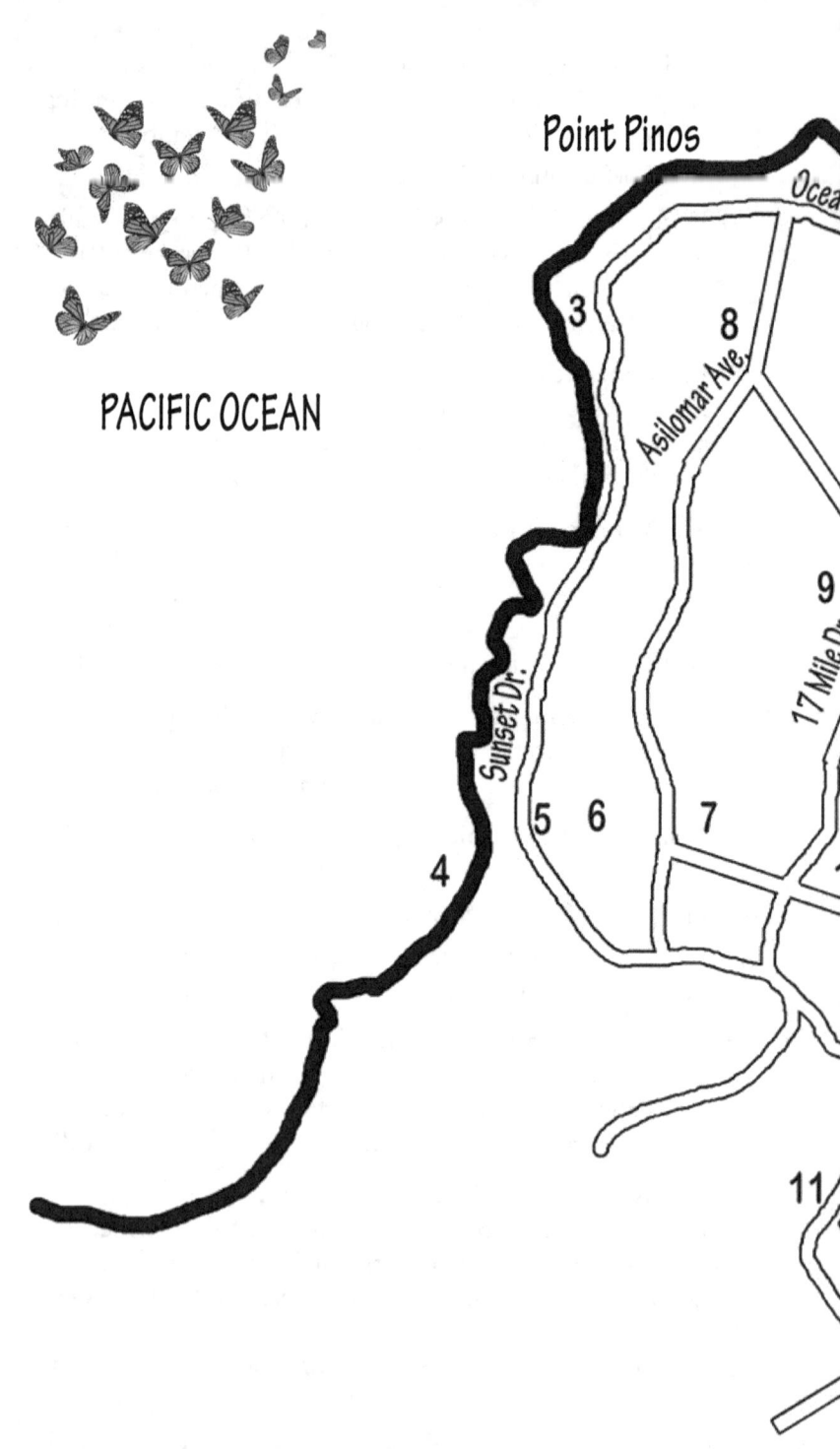

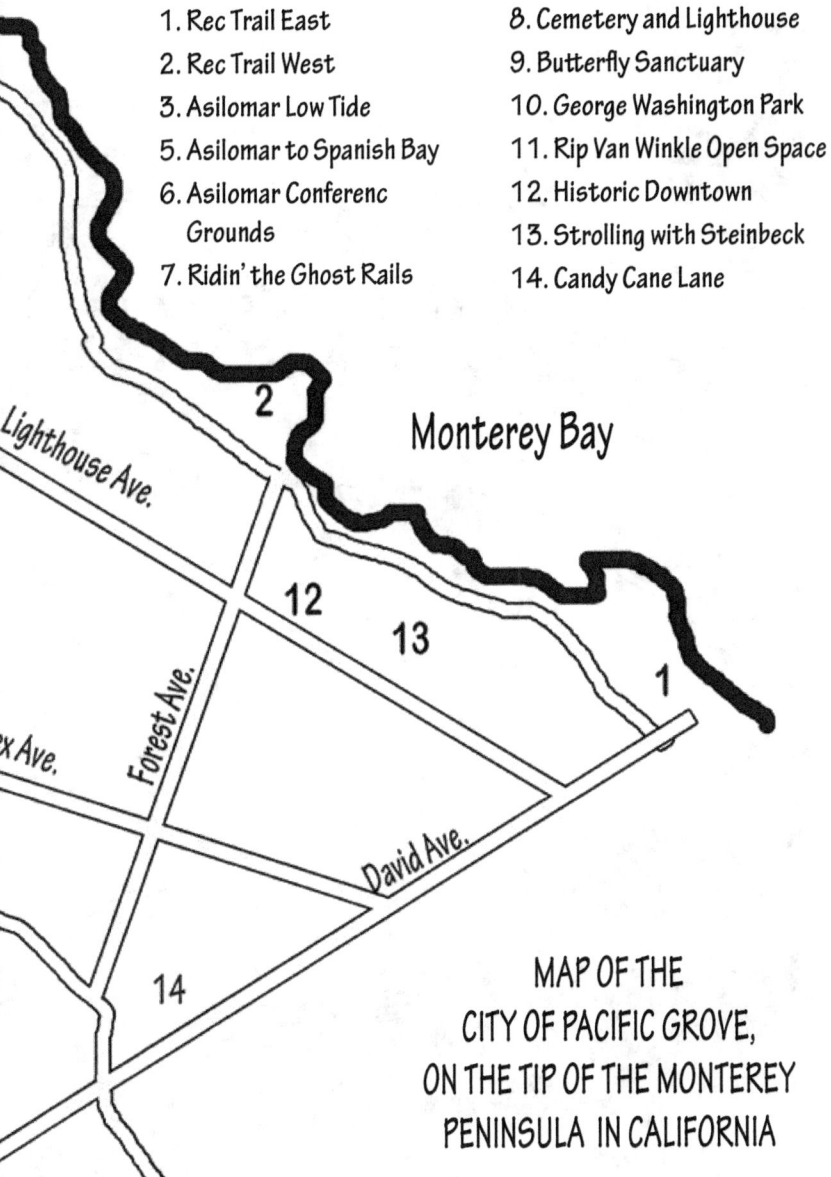

INTRODUCTION

Pacific Grove is known as Butterfly Town, USA, and America's Last Hometown. It was even honored by *Life* magazine as the nation's most romantic city.

With all due respect to civic boosters, they've overlooked the best slogan of all: Pacific Grove—The Perfect Walking Town.

Consider the climate, making outdoor activity a pleasure no matter the season. Our temperatures are rarely uncomfortably hot or bitterly cold, and on only a handful of days a year is it so wet and windy that it's impossible to set foot outdoors at some point during the day.

Pacific Grove is blessed with miles of walking paths, hiking trails, and city sidewalks, all safe and well-maintained. Your on-foot journeys through the town will take you past the home of a Nobel Prize laureate and Victorian houses both cute and majestic. Farther afield you'll find a lighthouse, a historic cemetery, and a conference center designed by the architect of Hearst Castle. Venture onto our shoreline Recreation Trail or into one of our parks, and you will be greeted with incomparable scenery, from the waters of Monterey Bay teeming with marine wildlife to urban forests, and even a butterfly sanctuary.

In short, we've got it all here, folks, spring, summer, fall or winter: fabulous weather, quaint Victorian cottages, tame wildlife (some might be a little too tame!), and more safe and easy paths than you could shake a walking stick at.

Though there is no central agency that rates hikes like they do movies, Pacific Grove's walks fall under the generally-accepted category of Easy: suitable for all ages and fitness levels, limited elevation gain, no rocky or uneven surfaces, three miles or shorter. Some are even accessible for those whose walk includes wheels—strollers, scooters, wheelchairs, surreys—and are so indicated.

As for equipment, all you really need are a pair of sturdy shoes and a water bottle. Be aware, though, that Pacific Grove's weather can be changeable. What starts out as a foggy morning can turn into a sunny midday and then again to a breezy late afternoon. Do like Mom said and dress in layers. For all but the most blustery winter days, a fleece hoodie or lightweight windbreaker should do it. A hat or cap with a brim is a nice accessory on sunny days, and don't forget the sunscreen!

In years of exploring Pacific Grove on foot, I am always intrigued at the many different types of hikers I encounter:

- The fitness walkers, getting in those 10,000 daily steps, burning those calories in our clean air.*
- The social walkers, teaming up with one or more friends or family for lively chatter while soaking up the beauty surrounding them.
- The studious walkers, noses buried in guidebooks or their phones, searching for landmarks, reading every plaque and signpost that they may run across.
- The nature walkers, reveling in identifying wildflowers, trees and shrubbery, whipping out binoculars to trace the flight of pelicans or the breaching of whales.
- The meditative walkers, using the combination of movement and an outdoor setting to quiet their minds, emptying themselves of all the cares of the world and become present to the natural world.

If you've guessed that I fit the latter type of walker, you win the prize. So, if you see me on the trail and say hello and I don't respond, I'm not intentionally being rude. I'm just far, far away, lost in my own world.

No matter what type of walker you are, what are you waiting for? Lace up your favorite pair of shoes, fill a bottle with water or other favorite beverage, select a destination from this book, and step out your front door.

Whether a long-time resident or a brand-new arrival, you, too, will discover that Pacific Grove, indeed, is The Perfect Walking Town.

The average person takes between 2,000 and 2,500 walking steps per mile as counted by a pedometer, fitness band, or phone motion sensor. Running steps have a longer stride length and you may take between 1,000 and 2,000 steps per mile. Hoeger WWK, Bond L, Ransdell L, Shimon JM, Merugu S. *One-Mile Step Count at Walking and Running Speeds.*

— RULES OF THE ROAD —

The Usual Cautions

- Be aware of your surroundings.
- Stay on the trail. No, you're not likely to get lost, and exposure to poison oak is relatively rare. But why trample on native plants or a tiny animal's home just for the sake of a short cut?
- Check yourself for ticks after walking in wooded areas.
- Don't hike alone, or at least tell someone where you're going and when you expect to return. (Not that I ever do this!)
- Avoid heavily forested parks during times of high winds—branches have been known to fall and strike the unwary.
- Best not to walk after dark, except in our downtown district or the Asilomar Conference Center grounds. Lighting is iffy to non-existent on the trails. Raccoons have been known to attack walkers of small dogs.

Mountain lion sightings at dawn or dusk are not unheard of. And, sadly, late night attacks, humans preying on other humans, have occurred on the Rec Trail. Only on rare instances, but still, better to play it safe.

Having gotten that out of the way, I will say that in twenty-five years and more of hiking, walking and rambling throughout Pacific Grove, about the worst thing that has happened is a pair of mud-soaked shoes after venturing out too soon after a rainstorm.

Dogs, Doobies and Drones

Pacific Grove is a very dog-friendly town and Fido is welcome on most of our trails as long as he's leashed. Exceptions—either no dogs allowed, or off-leash permitted—are noted on the individual walks. Of course, it's assumed you'll be a good citizen and pick up after your pooch. Many of our walking paths have dispensers with mutt mitts.

While we're on the subject of good manners, it should be noted that smoking in public is definitely frowned upon in our public spaces. If you absolutely must light up, do us all a favor and dispose of the butt in a proper receptacle. Please, I beg of you, do not just toss it on the ground and defile our beautiful little city. As for those "other" types smoking materials: yes, it is legal in California, but it's still against the law to light up a doobie in public, and that includes parks, beaches and city sidewalks.

Drones are not permitted in Pacific Grove unless you have a permit ($20 per day, must apply three days in advance) from City Hall. The Asilomar Conference Grounds does not have a specific drone policy, but state parks rangers do have the authority to regulate games and recreational activities, not only at the conference grounds but also at Asilomar beach and coast trail. If they feel the drone is interfering with visitor activities or endangering park resources, down it goes.

And finally…

Please resist the urge to feed our deer, raccoons, squirrels and seagulls, no matter how cutely they may beg. Instead just enjoy the engaging sketches of animals and plants by Judy Obbink and our digitally adapted photos by Patricia Hamilton.

WALKS, HIKES & RAMBLES IN BUTTERFLY TOWN, U.S.A.

#1 RECREATION TRAIL EAST

Every step makes a footprint.
—Chinese proverb

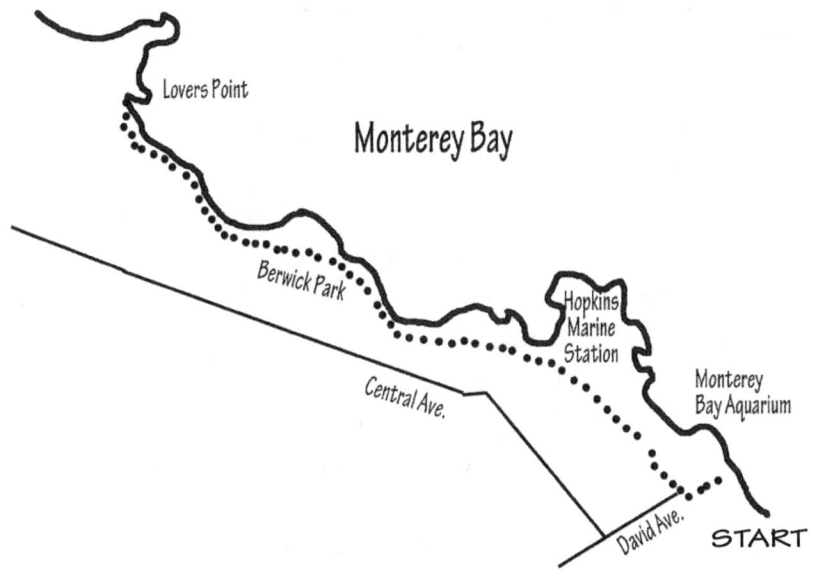

Monterey Bay Aquarium to Lovers Point

- 1.2 miles one way, 2.4 miles round trip/±2400–4800 steps
- Surface: asphalt or packed crushed granite, suitable for wheelchairs, strollers and scooters
- Public restrooms: At the beginning and end, on Hovden Way at the Monterey Bay Aquarium and at Lovers Point.
- Parking: Pay lots and metered street parking in the Cannery Row district, free, unlimited street parking along Ocean View Boulevard in Pacific Grove.

In Brief: *This beautiful, easy walk along the bluffs overlooking Monterey Bay is suitable for all ages and abilities, taking you from a world-class destination to a popular local park. On the way, you'll follow an old railroad bed as you pass by a harbor seal birthing beach and a popular selfie site.*

Convenient staircases and walkways connect Ocean View Boulevard with the Recreation Trail (known by locals as simply "Rec Trail") throughout this walk, so you really could start and end anywhere you please. But today, let's begin at 886 Cannery Row—the Monterey Bay Aquarium.

But wait—the *Monterey* Bay Aquarium? Isn't this supposed to be a book about Pacific Grove?

True enough. Technically, though, a small portion of the aquarium lies within the Pacific Grove city limits. The boundary runs right through the aviary, with everything to the west in the jurisdiction of Pacific Grove.

Beyond legalities, Pacific Grove can certainly claim ownership of the aquarium's origin story. It all started in 1977, when four Stanford University students studying at the **Hopkins Marine Station**—well within the boundaries of Pacific Grove—got to talking about their next-door neighbor, the abandoned ruin of the **Hovden sardine cannery**. Wouldn't it be a groovy location for an aquarium? As luck would have it, one of those marine biology grad students happened to have access to the Hewlett-Packard tech fortune.

Seven years later, this "wouldn't it be cool if …" fantasy became reality with the opening of the world-renowned **Monterey Bay Aquarium** on October 20, 1984. As the aquarium marketing folks like to say, they brought the fish back to Cannery Row.

◘ ◘ ◘

So, let us start our walk on the paved path that crosses David Avenue just up the hill from the aquarium entrance. Turn right, heading west.

The path is wide, flat and paved, ideal for bicycles, strollers and wheelchairs as well as those on foot, owing to its origin as a railroad bed for the **Del Monte Express** that served the area from the 1890s until the 1970s. More on the history of the train that used to run through Pacific Grove in Walk #7-Walkin' the Ghost Rails. For now, just be grateful that the civic leaders of Pacific Grove and Monterey had the foresight to convert the abandoned rail line into a walking and biking trail.

A word of caution is appropriate here: if you are on foot, stick to the dirt shoulder to avoid tangling with cyclists on the paved path, some of whom seem to think they're training for the Tour de France.

As you pass the aquarium staff parking lot and the tanks of the **Tuna Research and Conservation Center** (a joint project of the aquarium and Hopkins), keep your eyes out for a plaque on a boulder to your right. This small commemoration is all that is left of a **Chinese fishing village** that occupied this site in the late 1800s and early years of the 20th century.

The Chinese presence on the Monterey peninsula dates to the early 1850s, first settling in what is now Point Lobos State Reserve. Later, they moved to this site, then known as **Point Alones**. Here they established a thriving fishing village with a school, a temple, and small homes for dozens of families.

On May 16, 1906, a fire of mysterious origin burned the village to the ground, scattering the tight-knit community throughout the region. To this day, no one knows exactly how the fire started. Fingers of blame pointed at everyone from Monterey's Italian fishermen who wanted to quite literally burn out the competition, to Pacific Grove homeowners objecting to the smell of drying squid. As local lore would have it, the one man who knew the truth took the secret to the grave.

Today an annual Walk of Remembrance, usually on a Saturday in May, makes its way along the Rec Trail from the **Pacific Grove Museum of Natural History** to this site. This event features a traditional lion dance and is led by **Gerry Low-Sobado**, a fifth generation descendant of the village.

On the opposite side of Ocean View Boulevard, a large, white building is hard to miss. Built in 1927 as the **American Can Company**, it produced—you guessed it!—tin cans for all those canneries. Millions and millions of cans. When the sardine industry collapsed, the building was converted into a factory for making car seat covers for Chrysler. Old-timers recall the plant manager as always being able to find a job for any willing youth from his church.

Roughly the same time the aquarium opened in 1984, the old factory transitioned again, this time into a collection of restaurants and outlet shops known as the **American Tin Cannery**. As of this writing, the property's fate is uncertain. A proposal a couple of years ago to raze the building and construct a luxury hotel fell through. What's next in store is anyone's guess.

The facility to your right as we continue west is the aforementioned **Hopkins Marine Station**. Founded in 1892 by Stanford University as the first marine research lab on the U.S. Pacific coast, it was originally located at **Lovers Point**—the final destination of this walk—and moved to its current location in 1917. By the way, the Hopkins in the name refers to Timothy Hopkins, adopted son of railroad magnate Mark Hopkins and a major supporter of Stanford University during its early years. No connection to Johns Hopkins University.

By now, you've undoubtedly noticed the chain link fence that separates the Hopkins grounds from the Rec Trail. It's there for a good reason, to protect the colony of harbor seals basking on the Hopkins beach.

Wait—how do you know these are harbor seals and not sea lions? Simple. Harbor seals are spotted in colors of gray, black and tan, while sea lions have a dark, even coat. Sea lions can "walk" on their front flippers, while seals propel themselves on land by "scooching" along like large slugs. And if you can get close enough, you may notice that sea lions have external ear flaps, while seals have none.

Harbor seals are shy and spook easily, especially when they sense the presence of humans or their canines. They need safe, protected beaches like the one at Hopkins so they can haul out to rest and care for their young. They prefer to stay in the same location most of their lives (typically 25 to 30 years) and venture far afield only if necessary to find food (fish, squid, crustaceans) or a mate.

The beach at Hopkins is a popular place for these marine mammals to give birth and raise their pups. Breeding season is March through May. So, if you see a cluster of people peering through the fence, cell phone cameras aloft, a new pup may just be emerging from its mother's womb. Given some of our species' insatiable curiosity and craving for that perfect Instagrammable moment, it's easy to see why the fence is a necessity.

During pupping season, you'll probably encounter a volunteer in a blue **Bay Net** jacket. They're happy to answer your questions about the natural wonders of Pacific Grove, and will let you peer through their telescope at the seals, or even at a breaching whale out in the bay.

Further west on the path, beyond the Hopkins property, the city of Pacific Grove erects a temporary lattice fence to protect the pocket beach at the foot of Fifth Street during the breeding months. The intent is the same, to provide sanctuary for the newborns and their mothers from intrusive humans and their dogs.

This is as good a place as any to caution that getting too close to marine mammals like harbor seals, attempting 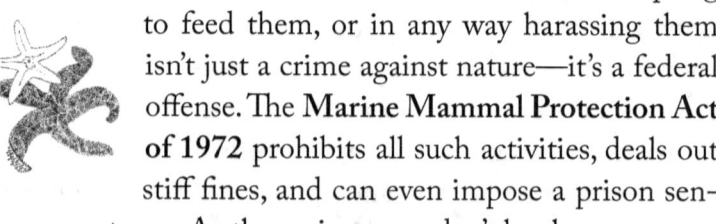 to feed them, or in any way harassing them isn't just a crime against nature—it's a federal offense. The **Marine Mammal Protection Act of 1972** prohibits all such activities, deals out stiff fines, and can even impose a prison sentence. As the saying goes, don't be that guy.

If you witness some knucklehead vaulting over the fence or otherwise giving our beloved harbor seals a hard time, call the **National Marine Fisheries Service** enforcement hotline, 800-853-1964. If the issue is an animal that seems to be in trouble, the place to call is the **Marine Mammal**

Center, telephone 415-289-SEAL, or email rescue@tmmc.org. Photos are especially helpful.

As we continue our journey west, our next landmark is a lovely expanse of green known as **Berwick Park**. This popular wedding spot is named for Edward Berwick, an Englishman who settled in Carmel Valley in the late 1800s and planted a large, prosperous pear orchard. He also had a home in Pacific Grove and served as a member of the Board of Trustees (today's City Council) and as mayor. His lasting contribution was to preserve the area of his namesake park and arrange for the planting of the lush lawn overlooking the blue waters of the bay.

Note: Dogs are not allowed in Berwick Park.

This lovely city park is home to two works of public art, each with intriguing histories.

"Life at the Top" is a bronze sculpture of a mother sea otter and her pup floating on a bed of kelp. Pacific Grove sculptor **Christopher Bell** created the work and was said to have spent hours scouting out the exact spot for the installation, with the blended blues of the water and sky providing the perfect backdrop. It was presented to the city by the **Pacific Grove Rotary** in 1994.

Sadly, this talented artist died young, in 1997, just three years after completing "At the Top." His work lives on in the "Butterfly Children" statue in front of the Pacific Grove Post Office, and here at Berwick Park.

In sharp contrast to Bell's subdued work of art are the colorful, can't-miss-'em, breaching whales—either a civic disgrace or a very cool example of pop art, depending on who you talk to.

It all started in January of 2016, when high winter winds broke off many of the major branches of two Monterey cypress trees that stood side-by-side. Rather than risk more falling branches, the city cut the trees down to two large stumps.

Along came Monterey attorney **John Bridges**, who noticed the resemblance to two whales leaping out of the water. The Rotary Club hired woodcarver **Jorge Rodriguez** to put his chainsaw to work and finish the transformation. According to most people connected with the project, the original plan was to leave the carved wood in a natural state—no artificial color.

Just one problem—the remains of the trees contained considerable rot, which Rodriguez and his crew filled with scrap wood and other materials. With neither stump now resembling a solid piece of wood, they felt they had no choice but to paint the thing.

The result has been called cartoonish, garish, even kitschy. One online wit dubbed them **"The Mambo Whales"** because they supposedly look like they're engaged in the Latin ballroom dance.

And yet—tourists love those colorful leaping whales,

turning them into quite possibly the
town's most popular spot for Facebook
and Instagram selfies.

Just past Berwick Park, the path splits, to the left continuing along the flat, paved railroad bed, and to the right a gentle incline and more amazing views of crashing waves. The right-hand fork is not paved, however. The path consists of packed, crushed stone, uneven and crumbly in places. Still, it should be doable for strollers and wheelchairs.

Weekday mornings around 10 o'clock it's not unusual on this section of the trail to encounter one of those "fit mommy" groups. Energetic, Lycra-clad young women pause every so often to do squats, leg lifts and arm exercises at the direction of their leader while their little ones snooze away in their strollers. How fortunate these tykes are to be growing up in a town as special as Pacific Grove, with clean air, safe streets, good schools, and surrounded by so much natural beauty. One can only hope that their children and grandchildren will be so lucky.

The two sections of the trail come back as one just in time to showcase another piece of public art. What was once a boring, blank retaining wall has been reborn as a 344-foot long mural depicting the history of Pacific Grove through the stories of four sets of early residents: the native **Ohlone**, **Rumsen** and **Esselen** tribes, the Chinese fishing families, the Japanese abalone divers, and the Methodist tent campers.

Officially known as the **Irene Masteller Mural**, after the **Pacific Grove Arts Commission** member who conceived the idea and raised the funds by private donations to bring it to life, the mural was completed in 1998 by Petaluma artist

Jon Ton. Ms. Masteller referred to it as a "wall of reconciliation," because of the focus on marginalized peoples often ignored by the history books. I especially like the band running along the top depicting the many birds, mammals, reptiles, insects and sea creatures that make their home in this part of the world, our own version of *The Peaceable Kingdom*.

Before we reach Lovers Point and the end of this walk, let us pause and recognize three remarkable women who play a large part in keeping this public resource as special as it is.

The fact is, you hardly ever see the tiniest bit of litter on the Rec Trail, an unheard of phenomenon for an out-

door venue that gets so much use by the public. No, it's not the city, nor the Boy Scouts—you can thank Lynn Mason, Susan Pierszalowski, and Lila Selden. Every day for thirty years, these women have been donning gloves and reflective vests, and walking the Rec Trail with grabbers and trash bags, cleaning up beer cans, liquor bottles, diapers, tissues, food wrappers, cigarette butts and dog poop.

Thirty years. Every day.

So let us finish the final two-tenths of a mile of this walk with the magnificent **Seven Gables Inn** to our left, the sparkling waters of **Monterey Bay** to our right, **Lovers Point** in front of us, and gratitude in our hearts.

LOVERS POINT BEACH AND PARK

SWAN BOAT REPLICA AND THE REC TRAIL

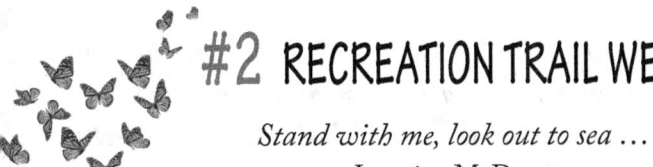

#2 RECREATION TRAIL WEST

Stand with me, look out to sea ...
—Lorraine M. Duncan

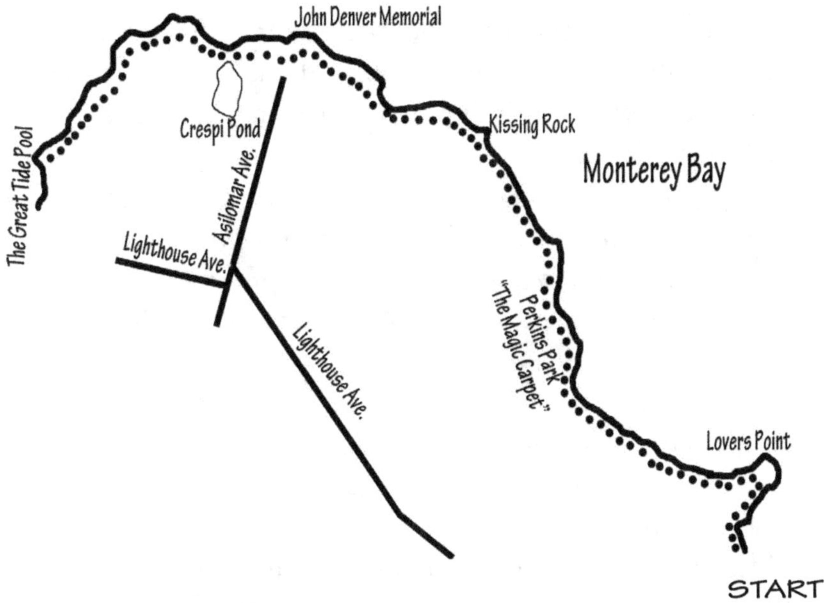

Lovers Point to the Great Tide Pool

- 1.5 miles one way, 3 miles round trip/±3000–6000 steps
- Surface: Dirt path, narrow in spots, plus short stretch on paved road
- Public restrooms: At Lovers Point Park and Crespi Pond
- Parking: Free with two-hour limit in city lots at Lovers Point, free and unlimited along Ocean View Boulevard and in the turnouts.

In Brief: *Breathtaking vistas of Monterey Bay and its abundant wildlife await those who tread this popular path. Numerous turnouts on Ocean View Boulevard with stairways and access paths make it easy to join this walk anywhere, or to do it in stages.*

As you might guess with a name like Lovers Point, this is an enormously popular spot for outdoor weddings. Likewise family picnics, charity walk-a-thons, and for those willing to brave the chilly waters, kayaking, surfing, scuba diving and wading.

Fun fact: Lovers Point is one of the few places on the West Coast where you can watch the sun rise over ocean waters. That's because it faces east across Monterey Bay, right in the direction of the sun as it peeks out above the Gabilan Mountains every morning.

Lovers Point may have been christened by the Methodists, but it owes much of its current topography to an early 20th century entrepreneur known as **William "Bathhouse" Smith**. He created the cove by dynamiting the rocky cliff, built the pier, and, naturally enough, a bathhouse. By 1912, Lovers Point boasted a bandstand, a merry-go-round, a saltwater swimming pool known as **The Plunge**, a Japanese teahouse, and even a silent movie theater. Gradually, these carnival-like entertainments fell victim to economic downturns, changing public tastes, and fire. The Plunge was the last to go, surviving into the 1970s. Talk to any Pacific Grove old-timer, and they'll share memories of learning to swim at The Plunge. Aging, rusted pipes spelled its doom, deemed too expensive to repair or replace. A sand volleyball court now stands where past generations learned the Australian crawl.

No history of Lovers Point, no matter how brief, is complete without a mention of **Julia Platt**. Hampered by the rampant sexism in the United States in the late 19th and early 20th centuries, she relocated to Germany to earn a doctorate in zoology, only to discover upon her return to U.S. soil that no university would hire her. So, she did the next best thing, becoming what was then referred to as a rabble-rouser—today, we'd call her an environmental activist.

In 1931, a private owner had erected a fence with locked gate barring access to Lovers Point. Enraged at this blatant attempt to deny the non-paying public access to this natural resource, Dr. Platt grabbed an ax, broke the lock and knocked down the fence. When some man asked her, "Who put you in charge?" or words to that effect, she responded by running for mayor—and winning. She next successfully lobbied Sacramento for a law granting Pacific Grove the right to manage its own shoreline. To this day, Pacific Grove is the only city in California granted that privilege.

Today, Lovers Point boasts two snack bars, the Beach Café and The Grill, and a sit-down restaurant, the Beach House, as well as a kiddie wading pool and a concession for renting kayaks, bicycles, and surreys.

Dogs are not permitted at Lovers Point. If Fido is part of your entourage, skip the park portion of this hike and stay on the Ocean View Boulevard sidewalk. Walk past the restaurant and pick up the Rec Trail on the northwest edge of the park.

◘ ◘ ◘

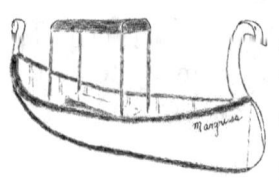

Our walk begins at the swan boat exhibit at the intersection of Ocean View Boulevard and Forest Avenue. These glass-bottomed boats operated for roughly 80 years, from the 1890s to the 1970s, offering visitors a view of the underwater wonders of the Lovers Point cove. This **swan boat replica** features heads salvaged from the original vessels. The name "Margruss" honors the couple who ran the concession for many years, **Margaret and Russell Sprague.**

From the swan boat exhibit, head down the asphalt slope past the snack bar, down the stairs and back up again, past the volleyball court, the kiddie pool, the restrooms, and the second snack bar, arriving at the lawn and picnic area. This vista may look vaguely familiar if you watched the second season of the HBO series *Big Little Lies,* as it was the location of the **Blissful Drip Café**. Alas, the enchanting, rustic outdoor coffee house was only temporary. Rumor has it, though, that the TV production company gave the set to the city when they'd finished filming. Where it's being stored and for what purpose—who knows?

Continue through the park on the paved path until you reach the bronze statue of a boy with a toy sailboat. The Pacific Grove High School class of 1944 raised the money and commissioned sculptor **Dorothy Fowler** to create **"Yesterday's Dream—Tomorrow's Memory,"** a poignant memorial to their classmates lost to war. The poem that accompanies the statue includes the line used at the beginning of this hike's description.

Bear to the right, around rock outcroppings and a stand of trees, to encounter a bench honoring one of the victims of the 9/11 attacks, **Suzanne Marie Calley.** Though not a resident of Pacific Grove at the time of the tragedy, she came here frequently to engage in her passion for scuba diving. You could say that Monterey Bay was her spiritual home.

Continue west as you exit the park, arriving at a dirt path that winds its way along the bluffs. Stop often to take in the amazing views, keeping your eyes out for playful sea otters and breaching whales. The first signs of the latter are often the spouts of water and air from their blowholes.

When the waters are calm and the skies clear enough that you can see the Santa Cruz side of the bay, I'm always struck as to how much this resembles a large lake. Gentle ripples of waves, seemingly surrounded by land—are you sure we aren't living on a lake?

Birds are abundant, including pelicans and the ever-present Western gulls. On the nearby offshore rocks, you'll undoubtedly spy Brandt's cormorants with their black wings outstretched. Unlike many other marine birds, their feathers are not water-repellant. Thus they spread their wings out to dry after diving—sometimes as deep as 40 feet—in search of food.

If the waters are especially calm, you may spot a slender,

snow white bird that appears to be performing the miracle of walking on water. This is an egret, a type of heron, balanced atop a bed of kelp, its eyes fixed patiently on the water for a tasty tidbit to swim by.

Along this stretch of the Rec Trail, you'll encounter numerous memorial benches, a place to pause to take in the scenery. This program of honoring departed loved ones has proved so popular, the city has declared the waiting list "indefinitely full." Perhaps that's okay—these folks have all of eternity to wait.

Don't be surprised if you meet one or more of our friendly ground squirrels, some so tame they might even attempt to crawl up your pants leg if you stand still for too long. Resist the urge to encourage this behavior, no matter how cute. Do not, I beg of you, feed them. You're not doing anyone any favors, neither for the animal nor for the other humans using the Rec Trail.

Next we arrive at a turnout at the foot of Sea Palm Avenue, the start of a section of the trail known as **Perkins Park**. A sign at the turnout commemorates **Hayes Perkins**, a remarkable gentleman who transformed a barren stretch of land into a "blaze of glory."

Perkins spent much of his life exploring the world and referred to himself as a "retired adventurer" when he settled in Pacific Grove in the 1940s. At the time, the major plant life on this part of the Rec Trail consisted of poison oak. Hayes took it upon himself to remove the noxious shrubs and replace them with the plants he'd seen while traveling in Africa: lilies, scarlet aloe, and especially *Drosanthemum floribundum*, better known as pink ice plant. The latter took especially well to the Pacific Grove climate, not even minding the occasional splashes of salt water from winter waves.

Before long, images of the **"magic carpet,"** the solid mass of pink blossoms against the blue waters of Monterey Bay, began popping up on postcards and in magazine articles extolling the natural beauty of the Monterey peninsula. A grateful city presented a plaque to Perkins in 1950. By all accounts a quiet and modest man, he simply said it had been a dream since boyhood to have "a beautiful garden by the sea."

Sadly, recent years have not been kind to the beloved and much-photographed local landmark, as it was hammered by the combined forces of a multi-year drought, city budget woes, and invasions of gophers and foxtails. What had once been a vast expanse of pink, pink and more pink in April and May, one of Pacific Grove's signature scenes, had degraded to struggling patches or in places simply gone. A corps of volunteers led by **Amy Colony** has come to the rescue by organizing clean-up days. The city council has ponied up funds to create a landscape maintenance plan for the magic carpet. With any luck, Perkins' dream of a "beautiful garden by the sea" will return as if …well …by magic.

The trail continues to **Esplanade Park** and a local landmark known as **Kissing Rock**. Not as you might think a place where teenagers go to neck, but rather an arch made of a common local rock geologically known as Santa Lucia granodiorite just offshore that some say resembles two human heads engaged in a lip-lock. To me, it has always looked more like two dogs touching noses, but whatever.

A landmark of a more somber nature is found at a turnout on the section of Ocean View Boulevard between Acropolis Street and Asilomar Avenue. A boulder with a bronze plaque commemorates the spot where singer/songwriter **John Denver** lost his life on October 12, 1997.

With his mop of blond hair, thousand-watt smile, and simple tunes that anyone could sing along with on the radio, Denver rocketed to stardom in the 1970s. He became one of the top entertainers of the decade and remains among the most popular male vocalists of all time.

He spent his final day playing golf with his celebrity pals at **Pebble Beach** and then practicing take-offs and landings from the Monterey airport in an experimental plane he'd taken possession of just the day before. The craft ran out of fuel and plunged into Monterey Bay, taking with it the sole occupant—John Denver. He was 53 years old. The National Transportation Safety Board ruled the cause to be a combination of the pilot's general inexperience with this particular aircraft and a faulty fuel selector handle.

By the time of the fatal crash, Denver's superstar status had faded, but his untimely death was still a major news story, with media vans and trucks choking the section of Ocean View Boulevard closest to the crash site while helicopters circled overhead. For viewers and readers around the world, not to mention Denver's legion of fans, it was the first time most had heard of a little California coastal town called Pacific Grove. In a macabre sort of way, it put us on the map.

A fan club known as **California Friends of John Denver** successfully petitioned the city council for permission to place a memorial at the turnout. On September 23, 2007, a bronze plaque was embedded into a granite boulder.

I well remember that fatal Sunday in October of 1997 as one of those gorgeous days we often are blessed with in early autumn: brilliant sunshine, warm temperatures, light breeze, no fog. I'd like to think that John Denver died doing something he loved, and that his final vision on this earth consisted of the peacock blue waters of the bay shimmering as if dusted with gold.

Past the John Denver memorial and west of Asilomar Avenue, the path temporarily disappears. To continue this hike, we must take to the paved road. Be sure to walk in single file, stay as close to the shoulder as you can, and watch out! You'll be sharing the road with bicyclists and automobiles. A lot of drivers will be admiring the scenery and not paying a whole lot of attention to us pedestrians.

Across Ocean View Boulevard is **Crespi Pond**, named for Juan Crespi, a priest who traveled with Gaspar de Portola and his small army in their explorations of Alta California for Spain in 1769 and 1770. Crespi kept detailed journals of these expeditions and wrote of the **"salty lagunas of Punta Pinos."** Quite possibly, one of his salt-water lagoons at **Point Pinos** could be this pond, now part of the **Pacific Grove Golf Links** and a popular hangout for Canada geese.

Just past Crespi Pond, the dirt path picks up again, winding through several vehicle turnouts and making a gradual shift from a westerly direction to south. We have reached Point Pinos, the southern edge of Monterey Bay. Our route no longer follows the relatively placid waters of the bay, but rather the crashing waves of the open ocean. Peering out into the water, it's no longer possible to see the opposite shore. Instead the vast waters of the Pacific lie before us, as far as the eye can see and beyond.

Just after making the turn, but before you arrive at two houses on the ocean side of the street, a short stretch of boardwalk leads to the **Great Tide Pool**—the end of this walk, and the start of our next adventure.

#3 ASILOMAR COAST TRAIL

It is a fabulous place ...
—John Steinbeck

The Great Tide Pool to Asilomar State Beach

- 1 mile one way, 2 miles round trip/±2000–4000 steps
- Surface: Boardwalk, packed gravel, loose sand
- Public restrooms: None
- Parking: Free and unlimited in turnouts and shoulders along Sunset Drive

In Brief: *Asilomar Coast Trail offers an easy and relaxing walk on the rocky bluffs overlooking the Pacific Ocean with stunning vistas of crashing waves.*

Much of this hike is on boardwalk or packed, crushed granite, suitable for strollers and wheelchairs, although the complete trail does involve a short distance on loose, sandy soil. If possible, time your walk to end at sunset, especially if you're a first-time visitor. No trip to the California coast is complete without watching the orange solar star dip slowly below the horizon across a vast expanse of blue/gray ocean. If you're especially lucky, perhaps you'll even be rewarded with the legendary "green flash."

This is another one of those hikes that can be joined anywhere, as numerous access paths connect the main trail with the parking turnouts.

◘ ◘ ◘

Today, let's begin at the Great Tide Pool, at a turnout just north of the T-intersection of Lighthouse Avenue and Sunset Drive. If you go past a house on the ocean side of the street, you've traveled too far.

A short boardwalk takes you to a sign identifying the Great Tide Pool, immortalized in John Steinbeck's *Cannery Row* as the spot where Doc did his collecting of marine life specimens to sell to colleges and universities. The quote at the start of this hike is from Chapter 6 of *Cannery Row*, in which Doc and Hazel, one of the "boys" from the Palace Flophouse, go on a collecting trip at this very spot. Steinbeck goes on to give a lengthy and lyrical description of the sea life teeming here: mussels and limpets, nudibranchs, starfish, and shrimp.

As tempting as it may be to follow in the footsteps of Doc and do some collecting of your own, do not yield to the temptation. Do not even think about collecting, nor poking

at, turning over, or otherwise disturbing the creatures you may encounter in our local tide pools. Besides it simply not being the right thing to do, the Great Tide Pool is part of the **Monterey Bay National Marine Sanctuary** and the **Asilomar State Marine Reserve**. Between the federal and state governments, activities like collecting are strictly regulated. Except for recreational hook-and-line fishing, you're not allowed to mess with the animals, even if your name is Ed "Doc" Ricketts. So pause at the sign to take a selfie or two, and then turn south to continue this walk.

After a few feet in a southward direction, the trail turns inland, as if heading back to the road. Not to worry, we won't end up on Sunset Drive. The detour is simply so that we hikers can skirt around the two homes on the ocean side of the street.

The southernmost home, a relatively modest-looking wooden structure vaguely in the Craftsman style, is the older of the two. Topographic maps of Pacific Grove show a structure at this location dating back to 1948, and the general look of the home reflects that vintage.

I can remember visiting Pacific Grove in the 1980s, and spotting the twin stone pillars at the driveway identifying **Rocky Shores**, and a huge, towering antenna indicating the home of a ham radio enthusiast. I marveled at the good fortune of this guy (I know, but let's face it—ham radio was almost exclusively a "guy" hobby) in having this unobstructed location for his transmitting tower, able to send a signal over thousands of miles of empty ocean. Then I would wonder about the messages he'd be receiving from Russia, Japan, Australia and beyond.

The northern house, an imposing granite multi-million

dollar mansion, dates only to 2010, and was built only after a struggle lasting at least ten years. It seems that decades ago, the city had allowed this stretch of spectacular ocean-side property west of Sunset Drive to be subdivided and zoned for residential use. Just one house, Rocky Shores, was built, but five other parcels—one to the north, four to the south—were just sitting there, legally awaiting development. By the 1980s, it appeared likely that five more homes would pop up on this incomparable scenic vantage point.

Once again, concerned citizens came to the rescue. Led by **Russell and Ellen Coile**, they turned first to the city council, urging them to purchase the land from the estate of the original owner of Rocky Shores. When that didn't pan out, they embarked on a fundraising campaign of their own, and were able to amass the money to buy and preserve the four parcels on the southern side. The fifth parcel, to the north, remained in private hands and after years of negotiation with the **Department of Fish and Game** and numerous other government entities, construction began. It and the original Rocky Shores are the only two homes in Pacific Grove located on the ocean side of the streets.

Luckily for us walkers, part of the deal included allowing the public trail to cross the driveway shared by the two homes. So we shall do just that, being respectful, of course, that these are private residences and staying strictly on the trail. Once past the driveway, it curves westward, taking us back to the windswept bluffs that give Rocky Shores its name.

As the dirt path merges into boardwalk, look at your feet and you'll see the names of the individuals, families and businesses that donated the funds to save the land you are now walking on from development. Though time, weather and hundreds of hiking shoes have worn down many of the names to the point of illegibility, it is still worthwhile to give thanks to those who made this possible. If not for them, we'd be walking on the shoulder of Sunset Drive, admiring expensive homes instead of crashing waves.

Continue south on the boardwalk to discover a most delightful feature, a wooden gazebo. This has got to be the most romantic spot on the Monterey peninsula, if not all of California, to watch a sunset. Just imagine the pounding of the waves, the tang of salt air, and the sun sending a final burst of golden light over the far horizon, while you cozy up in this gazebo with a special someone. If you sneak in a bottle of bubbly and discreetly raise a toast to life and love, I'll never tell.

As you continue south on this trail and other shoreline paths in Pacific Grove, you will undoubtedly notice bits of shell and crushed rock mixed in with the sandy soil, reminders of the native **Rumsen** tribes that once fished and hunted in this area. These remnants of old refuse dumping grounds are called **middens**, and are prized by archeologists for the information they yield about the diet and hunting methods used by these ancient peoples.

Throughout this walk, you will encounter walkways and stairs leading down to the pocket beaches dotted among the rugged outcroppings. These are a great place to relax with a blanket and a book, but keep in mind that these beaches do front on the open Pacific and the waves can be treacherous. As the saying goes, never turn your back on the ocean. Yes, you'll see people venturing far out onto the rocks, but, like, what are they thinking? Never a good idea, no matter how calm the sea may appear. If you have small children with their hearts set on dipping their toes into the ocean, far better to take them to the cove at Lovers Point.

California State Parks manages the Asilomar Coast Trail and has recently completed a project to address the threat of climate change and rising sea levels. Portions of the trail have been rerouted, taking it inland from the edge of the bluffs. They've also installed raised boardwalks to withstand incursions of ocean water. Previously, much of the trail consisted of loose, sandy soil or uneven gravel, so these improvements make this beautiful, easy path even more of a delight for walkers of all ages and abilities

The final leg of this walk is on packed gravel and ends at wide, sandy **Asilomar State Beach**—the end of one adventure and the beginning of the next.

#4 THE BEACH AT LOW TIDE

*My life is like a stroll on the beach,
as near to the ocean's edge as I can go.*
—Henry David Thoreau

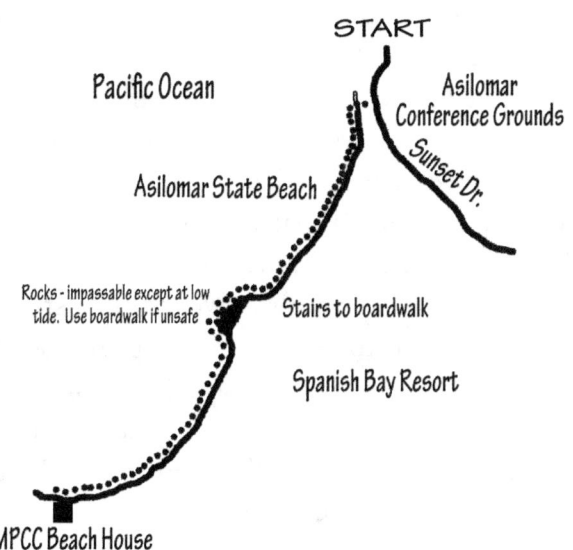

Northern end of Asilomar State Beach to southern end of Spanish Bay

- 1-1/4 mile one way, 2-1/2 miles round trip/±2500–5000 steps
- Surface: Depending on time of year, either packed, damp sand, or sand plus boardwalk. *Special wheelchairs designed for use on the beach are available for free checkout at the nearby Asilomar Conference Grounds. Details and reservations: 831/372-8016.*
- Public restrooms: None
- Parking: Free and unlimited on shoulder of Sunset Drive

In Brief: *The low-tide walk is a glorious little adventure right on the damp sand, taking you along two beautiful white sand beaches, best done in early fall.*

We're going to the beach! We're taking off our shoes and squishing our toes in the wet sand. We're going to feel the chilly waters of the Pacific caressing our ankles. We're going to walk on land that is usually underwater, exploring territory that is normally accessible only from the boardwalk on the bluffs above us—how cool is that?

What I love about the beach in general, and our local beaches in particular, is that they are never the same. You can visit every day, and each day will seem slightly different. In the winter, huge storm waves will strip most, if not all, of the sand right from the beach, exposing the rock lying just underneath. Not to worry, the sand is in a holding pattern right offshore and will return in the spring. Throughout the spring and summer months, the sand covers the rocks and slowly builds a dense, thick layer, at its peak in early fall. Combine that with an exceptionally low tide in the daylight hours and you've got the perfect conditions for a special walk.

Most weather apps and newspaper weather reports will include the day's high and low tides. Vendors who rent kayaks, surfboards and wetsuits are another source of local tide information, as are the websites tideschart.com and surfline.com. What you're looking for is a *minus tide* happening in the daylight hours. What's a minus tide? Basically it's any tide that is less than the mean low tide—in other words, a really, really low tide. On printed tide tables, they're usually indicated in red ink. Minus tides take place all year 'round, but fluctuate depending on the position of the moon and its gravitational pull on the earth. Lucky for us, early fall often sees minus tides occurring during the afternoon and early evening hours—just in time for the seasonal sand build-up. Adding to our good fortune: those eight or so weeks from mid-September to early November are usually the nicest time of the year on the Central Coast, weather-wise, with little fog and giving us warm temperatures, blue skies and light breezes. It's our true summer, ideal for a walk on the beach.

Now, you can do this walk pretty much any time of the year during any tidal condition, except, perhaps, when unusually strong winter waves really have removed every grain of sand. So except for that special time in early autumn when conditions line up perfectly, you'll need to do at least part of the hike on the boardwalk up on the bluffs.

◘ ◘ ◘

We'll start this walk at the northern end of Asilomar beach by carefully picking our way down the stone steps shown on page 46. If this pathway looks too treacherous, or you're in one of the Asilomar beach wheelchairs, there's a sand trail with a gentle slope further south on Sunset Drive.

I like to wear sturdy sandals on this particular walk, footwear I can easily kick off and carry and then slip back on, depending on changing conditions. And lest you think walking on the beach is going to be a chore, like trudging through a sandy desert, have no fear. Once the sand is wet, it packs down quite solidly. And yet, it also retains a bit of "spring," much like a wooden dance floor. It's actually quite comfortable and easy on the joints.

We're at the foot of the steps or the bottom of the sand walkway. Make your way across the beach towards the ocean until the dry sand—white, with grains so fine it feels like treading through powdered sugar—becomes damp. Now, if this is a time of a very low tide in the fall, you should see a wide expanse of wet sand, perhaps covered with an inch or two of water, with the waves breaking far beyond.

So … start walking! There's no marked trail when the path is usually underwater, folks. Just head south, with the ocean to your right and land to your left and you will not get lost, I promise.

Here at the northern end of the beach are rock outcroppings and examples of the **tide pools** for which Pacific Grove is well-known. This is a good place to issue a reminder as to how this section of coastline is protected by both the **Monterey Bay National Marine Sanctuary** and the **Asilomar State Marine Reserve**. Collecting is a big no-no. I cringe every time I see children with buckets in hand wading into the tide pools, knowing full well that whatever critters they might pick up and put in those pails—hermit crabs, limpets, starfish—will undoubtedly die before these kids even arrive home. Collect with your camera and leave these sea creatures to live to see another day.

If you're making this walk in the fall, before the first storms arrive, the shoreline will probably be relatively clean of seaweed and other debris. Once the first storm waves arrive, though, they will deposit large piles of kelp onto the sand. This is a natural phenomenon, the kelp beds being ripped from their rocky holdfasts and flung up on the shore—sometimes with rocks still attached. I was once stopped on a beach stroll by someone who was obviously not from around here, quite indigent that the beach wasn't clean enough for her standards, wondering why we Californians didn't rid our beaches of this stinky mess. I did my best to explain about letting nature take its course, that decay is a normal part of the life cycle, etc., etc., but she wasn't buying it. Oh, well. I happen to think beach wrack has its own particular beauty.

At times, you may find this beach littered with tiny blue creatures with little "sails" sticking up. Scientific name *Velella velella*, they are more popularly called by-the-wind sailors or sea rafts. These hydrozoa live on the surface of the ocean, feeding on plankton. With no means of locomotion of their own, they are easily influenced by the wind—hence the name. Depending on the wind speed and direction, thousands upon thousands of them may be tossed to their deaths on the beach. When this happens, beach-goers inevitably call the Asilomar rangers, or the **Monterey Bay Aquarium**, distressed about what appears to be a die-off of an entire species. No, they are told, it's another natural phenomenon, not to worry. Eventually, they'll dry out and crumble to dust, the life cycle continuing.

Asilomar is a very popular surf spot, so if the wave conditions are right, you'll undoubtedly see several dozen in their black wetsuits and on their boards bobbing in the lineup. Pause for a moment to watch one of these talented dudes or dudettes carve up a wave.

Shore birds are likewise quite fond of Asilomar, especially when the tide is out. Tiny sanderlings and plovers will wade in the shallow water, as well as avocets with their stilt-like legs and long, narrow beaks, perfect for poking through the wet sand in search of a treat.

With the wide expanse of glossy sand shimmering in the sunlight, sometimes walking on the beach at low tide almost feels like skating, as if I'm skimming across the thin slick of water—but then, I'm a girl with a vivid imagination.

A word about dogs. The northern part of the beach is under the control of **California State Parks** and while dogs are welcome, they must be leashed. The state park boundary is roughly just south of where a creek runs into the beach. This seasonal creek is usually dry except right after a rainstorm, but you can see its course by the green shrubs in a low-lying swale just before a row of dunes. South of the state park boundary is nominally under the control of the **Pebble Beach Company**, but in reality it's no man's land when it comes to our best friends. Lots of folks allow Fido to run off-leash and no one seems to care. Just use your usual good judgment when it comes to your canine's behavior when given this level of freedom.

A point of rocky land and rugged outcroppings in the ocean mark the southern end of Asilomar beach. But if the sands and tides are right—in other words, a minus tide in the fall—you may be able to walk around the point. This could require a bit of wading to make your way around some of the rocks, perhaps getting as much as calf-deep in the chilly Pacific. Other times, the sand has built up sufficiently and the tide is far enough out to make your way around the point without getting anything wet beyond the bottoms of your feet.

Before beginning to pick your way around the rocks to the far side, take a moment to assess the general situation and make a wise decision. If the waves are high, crashing against the rocks right along the shore, or if a huge bank of dead kelp has built up, don't do it. If you're making this walk at any time other than autumn during a low tide, don't even think about it!

There's always a Plan B. In this case, it involves heading

up a stairway and path near the end of the beach to take you to the boardwalk described in walk #5-Over the Boardwalk. Turn to your right and continue high and dry on the boardwalk until you reach the southern end of the rocky point. The boardwalk ends at the parking lot at **Spanish Bay,** where you can once again walk across the beach and continue your trek on the sands of low tide, continuing south.

If at all possible, I like to make the venture around the point while actually down at beach level at least once every fall season. There's just something about being in a place accessible only a few weeks out of the year, a tiny bit of adventure and hint of danger. Once around the point, you'll end up on the same section of beach as our fellow hikers who took the boardwalk route.

This particular stretch of sand was originally known as **Moss Beach,** apparently because early European explorers mistook the dead kelp that gets tossed up onto the beach in the winter months as moss. I've seen old topographic maps that refer to both this beach and Asilomar as Moss Beach. With the proximity to the Spanish Bay resort, most folks seem to call this Spanish Bay Beach. Just to make things even more confusing, some in the surf community refer to the section of Asilomar south of the state park boundary as Spanish Bay, and this particular beach by its traditional name of Moss Beach. But hey—we've got the same sand, surf and sun. As the bard would say, what's in a name?

Congratulate yourself for having gotten past the gates of the exclusive Pebble Beach resort without paying the entry fee as you continue walking south on the beach. You will notice the landward side of the beach covered with small,

smooth rocks, most round or oblong. Surfers refer to this section of beach as **"Cobblestones,"** and the stones have proven enormously popular with visitors who like to engage in rock-stacking, turning this section of beach into a veritable sculpture garden.

Our low tide walk concludes at the southern end of **Spanish Bay Beach** (or Moss Beach, if you prefer), in front of a Mediterranean-style building with the traditional white stucco walls and red barrel tile roof. Though somewhat modest by Pebble Beach standards, the location and picture windows facing the ocean give it luxury status. Topographic maps show a structure at this location as early as 1941 and my recollection of doing this hike for the first time back in

the 1990s is of a private home. I'd peek through the windows from afar, watching the occupants going through their perfectly normal routine of cocktail hour, television-watching or newspaper-reading. I always hoped they realized their good fortune in having a home in such a special place. The building is now part of **Monterey Peninsula Country Club** and seems to be used mostly for weddings.

We've now reached another point of land, with rocks too difficult to traverse on foot in even the most favorable tide conditions. This is our signal to turn around and make our way back to the starting point at Asilomar, either on the boardwalk or, if our luck continues, walking on the beach the entire way.

#5 OVER THE BOARDWALK

Poppies, golden poppies, gleaming in the sun ...
  —Leila France

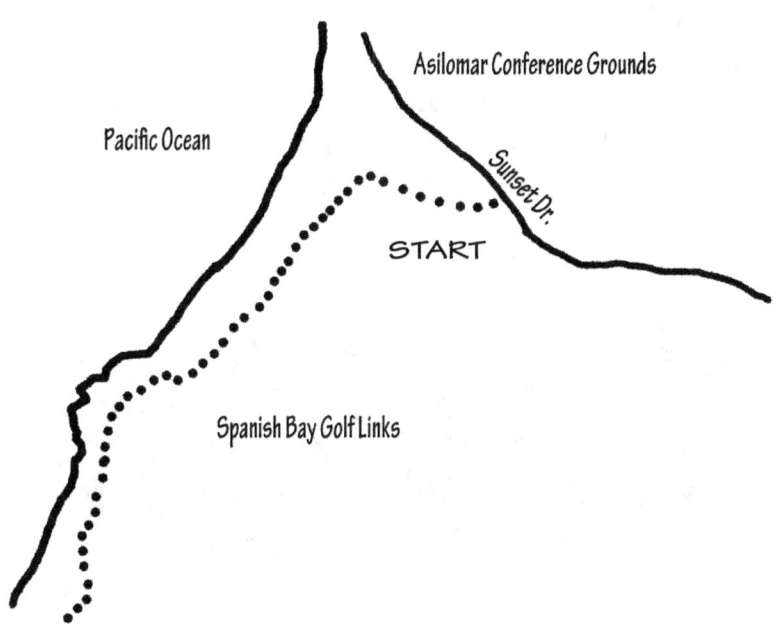

Sunset Drive to the Spanish Bay parking lot

- 3/4 of a mile one way, 1-1/2 miles round trip/±1500–3000 steps
- Surface: Mostly boardwalk, plus short stretches on dirt path and loose sand
- Public restrooms: None
- Parking: Free and unlimited on Sunset Drive

In Brief: *A mostly easy walk along the shoreline bluffs on a well-maintained boardwalk. A few yards over a relatively steep sand dune might elevate this walk from easy to moderate status.*

For years when I was working a traditional day job, this walk was my reward on a Friday afternoon. Just long and brisk enough—one half hour to forty-five minutes—to make me feel as if I'd had a decent workout after sitting at a desk in front of a computer all day. With fresh ocean breezes and vistas of breaking waves, it provided the perfect bridge between the workaday world and the promise of relaxation and fun on the upcoming weekend.

To start this walk, you'll drive past the beach at Asilomar on Sunset Drive, and ditch the car along the dirt shoulder. If you reach the Beachcomber motel, you've gone too far. The trailhead will be at the northern end, the start of what is usually a line of parked cars.

The first few yards are on a packed dirt path and include a bridge that crosses a seasonal creek. Usually dry or with stagnant liquid, the water will move along quite rapidly following a good, long downpour.

Beyond the bridge and just as the boardwalk begins, you'll encounter that sand dune I warned you about. We're now in territory under the jurisdiction of the Pebble Beach Company. So if you want to get technical, this isn't really a Pacific Grove hike, as pretty much all of it is outside the town boundary. But the parking area along Sunset Drive is definitely part of Pacific Grove, so we're going to claim the walk as our own.

At any rate, the Pebble Beach Company deserves our thanks for maintaining and improving the boardwalk, including a recent project to lay new planks up and over the sand dune, turning a dreary slog into a still challenging but much more pleasant walk. The dune provides a workout that will get your heart and lungs pumping. Once on the downward side, congratulate yourself for having already completed the most difficult portion of this walk.

Once up and over the sand dune, the boardwalk becomes visible and guides you along gentle curves and rolling hills for the rest of the way. I might add the Pebble Beach Company is diligent about replacing broken or rotted boards.

To your left you'll see the **Spanish Bay Golf Links** and to your right, dunes, then beach, then ocean as far as the eye can see. In the springtime, **California poppies** grow in

profusion along this stretch of the trail. Whenever I see a clump of the pretty orange blossoms, I am reminded of the ditty all of us California kids—at least, those of us of a certain age—learned in elementary school:

Poppies, golden poppies, gleaming in the sun,
Closing up at evening when the day is done.
Pride of California, flower of our state
Growing from the mountains to the Golden Gate.

This simple little blossom was put to good use by the native tribes, who used poultices and tinctures derived from the poppy for everything from killing lice to easing toothaches to calming babies. The Spanish explorers dubbed

the flower *copa de oro* (cup of gold). As some native tribes told a legend of poppies that deposited the gold in the earth that the Yankees finally discovered in 1848, perhaps those Spaniards were on to something.

In 1913, after years of lobbying by the **California State Floral Society,** botanists and various other garden clubs, Governor Pardee signed a bill making the California golden poppy the official state flower.

Roughly at the halfway point of this walk, we will reach a rustic stairway and path leading to the beach. For this particular walk, however, we'll stick with the boardwalk.

Past the beach access, the trail makes a slight turn as we make our way around the rocky point that separates the Asilomar and Spanish Bay beaches. Some folks swear they have spotted the remnants of shipwrecks at this rugged spot. No question, ships ran afoul of these hazards during the 1800s and early 1900s as they searched for Monterey Bay in the fog, but I've never seen a wreck, and I make this walk *a lot*. I'm guessing what they're really seeing are partially submerged jagged rocks that resemble a ship's prow. Still, this rocky point does seem to exude a certain spiritual energy, this churning, crashing, roaring meeting of land and sea.

A little further along, the boardwalk makes a T intersection. If you were to take a 90 degree turn to your left, the trail would deliver you to the Spanish Bay hotel. But that's not our destination, at least not today. Continue more or less straight ahead, on the boardwalk that runs along the shoreline bluffs.

I well remember one of those late Friday afternoons after work, when the trail was relatively deserted. Up ahead were two men smoking cigars and clutching glass tumblers containing a brown liquid. They had obviously just wandered down to the water from **Spanish Bay**, possibly here on a business conference or a sales incentive junket. They studied me as I strode past, and one of them said in a thick Texas drawl, "Honey, y'all are workin' way too hard." I laughed and replied to the effect that, "No, this is my reward for working too hard all week."

After a few more easy up-and-downs on the boardwalk over the sand dunes, the trail ends at the parking lot for the Spanish Bay stop on the **17-Mile Drive**. Of course, you could go on—the trail picks up on the far side of the car park, and could take you all the way to **Point Joe** and **Bird Rock**. But, this is a book about Pacific Grove hikes, not Pebble Beach, so we shall end here, making a 180 and going back the way we came.

#6 ASILOMAR CONFERENCE GROUNDS

... the spirit of Asilomar, a something hard to define; yet a something that everyone should possess.
—From *The Pie Rat Newsletter*, 1931

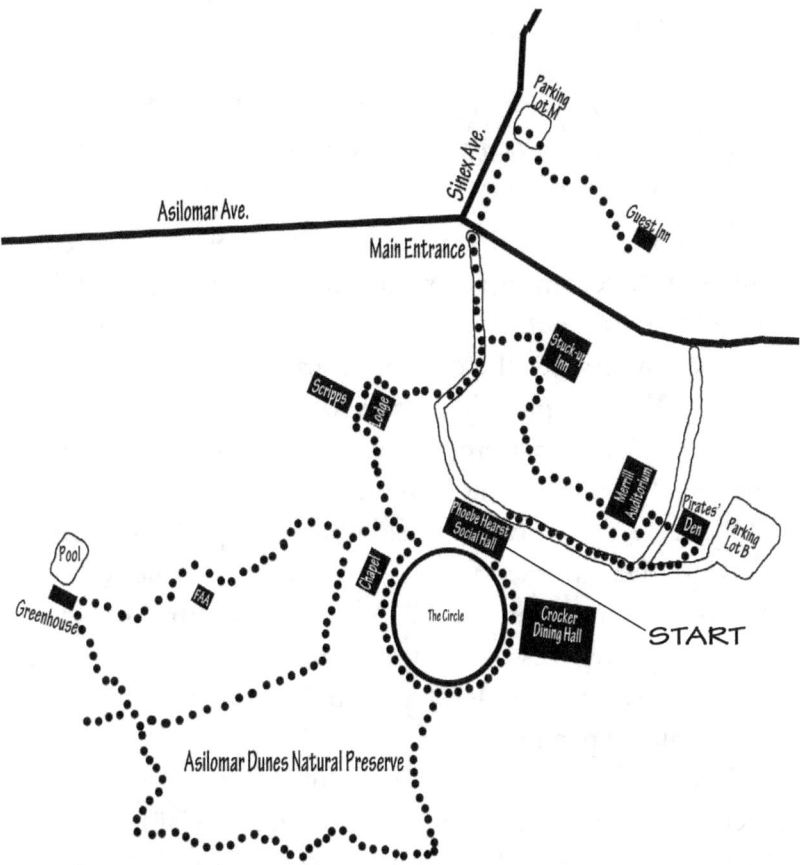

Asilomar Conference Grounds, 800 Asilomar Avenue

- 1 mile total/±500–2000 steps. In sections: Julia Morgan tour, 1/4 mile. Side trip to Guest Inn, 1/4 mile. Side trip to Asilomar Dunes Preserve, 1/2 mile.
- Surface: Mostly brick pavers and boardwalk, some asphalt, with mild to moderate elevation changes

- Public restrooms: Inside Phoebe Hearst Social Hall
- Parking: Free and unlimited in conference center parking lots or on the dirt shoulder on Asilomar Avenue
- Dogs must be leashed and are not allowed inside buildings

In Brief: *Explore the work of famed architect Julia Morgan in a beautiful natural setting, with optional side trips to a cottage with a Steinbeck connection and over the sand dunes.*

Asilomar traces its roots to the **Young Women's Christian Association,** an organization that sprang up at the turn of the 20th century to assist the thousands of girls who were streaming into the nation's cities in search of a better life. The YWCA provided a safe shelter and job training. In California, several prominent society women, including **Phoebe Apperson Hearst,** mother of newspaper tycoon **William Randolph Hearst,** held leadership positions in the YWCA. These women wanted a permanent venue to hold leadership retreats, and in 1913, the **Pacific Improvement Company,** predecessor to the **Pebble Beach Company,** donated 30 acres of undeveloped land on the western tip of the Monterey peninsula.

The YWCA hired **Julia Morgan,** the first woman to receive an architect's license in the state of California, to design the buildings. Next on their to-do list—find a name for the new retreat center. The YWCA held a contest that drew hundreds of entries. A Stanford student, Helen Salisbury, came up with a winner when she combined two Spanish words for a new, made-up name: "asilo" for refuge and "mar" for the sea. Thus came Asilomar's nickname,

"refuge-by-the-sea." On August 7, 1913, Asilomar was dedicated in an elaborate ceremony and pageant attended by some 2,000 people.

For the next 20 years, Asilomar perked along as a summer retreat for YWCA leaders, most of them college-age women, and a camp for girls. In the off season, they rented out the grounds to organizations and businesses wishing to hold conferences, much like today. But hard times came during the **Great Depression**, and Asilomar was no longer economically sustainable. In 1934, the YWCA national board voted to close the camp and put the property up for sale. There were no takers.

For a while, various entrepreneurs leased Asilomar to run as a private hotel. In **World War II**, it housed military families. Some years, it simply sat empty.

When word got out in the early 1950s that a glass company was sniffing around the Asilomar dunes as a potential site for a sand mine similar to the plant next door at Spanish Bay, it was "game on" for the local citizenry. They rose up in outrage and successfully lobbied Sacramento to purchase

Asilomar as a state park. In 1956, the YWCA officially turned over the conference grounds to the **Department of Parks and Recreation.**

The 1960s saw a period of expansion, with additional acreage purchased and new meeting space and overnight rooms constructed. While not exact copies of Julia Morgan's Arts and Crafts style, the new buildings did follow the same rustic, outdoorsy theme. It was during the 1960s that the conference center made the leap across Asilomar Avenue, growing to its present 107 acres.

For a time, the city ran the conference operations; later it was handed over to a nonprofit corporation under the direction of the state. Since 1997, private, for profit concessionaires have operated the conference facilities, but the buildings and grounds are still part of the **State Parks** system.

Today, Asilomar continues to host hundreds of conferences, big and small, every year. It's also a popular venue for family reunions and weddings.

◘ ◘ ◘

LOBBY OF THE PHOEBE HEARST SOCIAL HALL.

To begin the Julia Morgan section of our walk, make your way to the **Phoebe Hearst Social Hall** at the center of the conference grounds. I usually park in Lot B next to the sand volleyball court and in back of **Pirates' Den**, making the short walk to the main hall, but you can also access Asilomar via bicycle or MST bus. There's a stop across the street from the entrance pillars, in front of the motels.

Morgan is best known for having designed **Hearst Castle**, but she left her imprint on many commercial structures and private homes throughout California—more than 700 in her 47-year career. Evidence of her residential work can be seen at a home at 104 First Street here in Pacific Grove. Asilomar represents the largest collection of her **Arts and Crafts**-style work in one place.

Phoebe Hearst Social Hall, the original administration building, always reminds me of one of those grand lodges from the 1920s, like Yosemite's Ahwahnee Hotel, what with its soaring height, heavy redwood beams and massive granite fireplace. It's one of my favorite spots in Pacific Grove, an

VIEW OF THE CIRCLE FROM THE TERRACE.

ideal venue for curling up with a book by the fire on a cold, blustery day or relaxing with a glass of wine from **Phoebe's Café** out on the terrace when the weather is pleasant.

This building essentially serves as the lobby and includes the check-in counter, a gift shop, the aforementioned café, an antique piano, pool tables, and restrooms. Be sure

MARY ANN CROCKER DINING HALL

to stop at the information desk and help yourself to the free brochures about Julia Morgan, the Asilomar dunes and its wildflowers. Our Julia Morgan tour follows the one described in greater detail in the brochure, so it's definitely worth picking up. Also check to see if any guided tours are being offered.

From the terrace, bear to your left, around the plot of undeveloped land known as **The Circle** to find the **Mary Ann Crocker Dining Hall**, built in 1918 to replace what had been large tents. If the Crocker name is vaguely familiar, think back to the Big Four who built the transcontinental railroad. Mary Ann was **Charles Crocker**'s wife, and the family donated money for the construction of the dining hall.

Like the other buildings that Morgan designed for

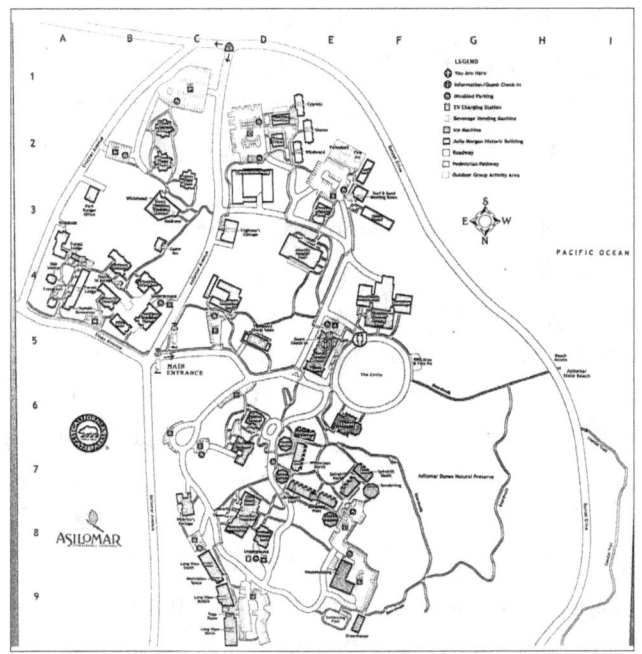

ASILOMAR DIRECTORY OUTSIDE THE DINING HALL

Asilomar, this one reflects her decision to use natural materials to blend with and complement the local terrain: fireplaces of granite blocks, beams and posts of raw wood, sometimes with bark still attached. Large windows let in light and create the illusion of being one with nature.

Continue around The Circle, reaching the **Grace Dodge Chapel** directly opposite the dining hall. Like so many smart and capable women of the Victorian era, **Grace Dodge** was denied the opportunity to attend college or take an active role in her wealthy family's business affairs. So she did the next best thing, throwing herself into philanthropic pursuits to improve the lives of women. She was elected the first national president of the YWCA, and although she never actually visited Asilomar, the chapel is named in her honor.

If no groups are meeting, you should be able to venture inside. Pause to admire the jagged stonework jutting from the window bays, and the biblical inscription carved and decorated with gold leaf and surrounded by a pattern of shells.

From the chapel, follow an asphalt road uphill in a northerly direction. The **Visitor's Lodge** was built in 1915. As the name would suggest, its purpose was to house visitors, guests who wanted accommodations more luxurious than a canvas tent.

Continue a few more yards uphill. **Scripps Lodge** was dedicated to a pioneering woman journalist, **Ellen Browning Scripps**. She and her brother created a newspaper empire in the late 1800s and amassed a large fortune, most of which she gave away in her later years. You may have seen the family name on numerous institutions that she endowed in Southern California: Scripps College, Scripps Institute of Oceanography, and Scripps Research Institute, just to name a few. She admired the work of the YWCA and donated money to purchase additional land at Asilomar. The building that bears her name was constructed in 1927 to house the year-round conference attendees.

Make a 180, head back downhill, cross the road, and head up the inclined path as if making for the main entrance of the conference grounds. At the right is a 1918 building with the unusual name of **Stuck-Up Inn**. During the early years of the summer camp, the YWCA hired young women to carry out necessary housekeeping chores like cleaning and laundry. This building was their dormitory. Several of these young women were heard complaining of the menial nature of the work, causing one listener to say, "You're just a bunch of stuck-ups." The name, well … stuck. Instead of taking

MARY S. MERRILL AUDITORIUM

offense, the young women embraced it as a badge of honor.

A path with a downhill slope and heading in a southwest direction leads to one of the most impressive buildings at Asilomar, the **Mary S. Merrill Auditorium**. Dedicated in 1928 to the memory of one of the Bay Area philanthropists who helped fund Asilomar, it is the last Julia Morgan design to be built at the conference grounds.

Continue south, crossing another road, and arrive at the delightfully named **Pirates' Den**, built in 1923 to house the young men who worked at the summer camp. They referred to themselves as pirates in the tradition of **Robert Louis Stevenson**, going so far as to dress up as buccaneers and "raid" the dining hall, much to the presumed amusement of the young female guests. Arrr! In later years, their name transitioned to **"Pie-Rats"** due to the young rapscallions' fondness for filching pies from the kitchen.

Turn around at the Pirates' Den and walk on the brick pavers that run along the road to complete the loop back to the social hall.

Steinbeck Side Trip

From the **Phoebe Hearst Social Hall**, head uphill on the main road to the entrance. Pass through the iconic granite pillars and cross Asilomar Avenue to reach the newer, 1960s-era addition to the conference grounds. Walk up Sinex Avenue. Turn right into Parking Lot M. Walk across the lot, between two buildings called **Hearth** and **Kiln**, then between **Embers** and **Afterglow**. Continue in a southerly direction until you reach an unassuming building with the prosaic name of **Guest Inn** sitting out there by its lonesome.

The conference grounds expanded to the east side of Asilomar in the 1960s. But before that—from the 1930s into the 1950s—**John Steinbeck's** sister and brother-in-law, **Esther and Carrol Rodgers**, lived in what is now called **Guest Inn**. Steinbeck spent time there with his second wife, **Gwyn Conger**, and in the 1940s escaped his growing fame at that modest sanctuary. He was quoted as saying he wrote portions of *The Log from the Sea of Cortez* in a cabin hidden in a pine woods amidst sand dunes. Could this be that cabin? You be the judge.

But seriously ... Guest Inn? Surely the author of works with such evocative place name titles as *Tortilla Flat*, *Pastures of Heaven* and *East of Eden* would have created a name a bit more imaginative, don't you think?

At this point, you may choose to either turn around and return to **Phoebe Hearst Social Hall** the way you came, or continue on this sidewalk, past the **Mott Training Center**, across Asilomar Avenue, back down the road past **Pirates' Den** and **Merrill Hall**, and return to the starting point in a loop.

Asilomar Dunes Natural Preserve Side Trip

The arrival of what we might call civilization was not kind to the 480 acres of sand dunes that once stretched from **Point Pinos** in Pacific Grove to **Point Joe** in Pebble Beach. Logging, grazing, sand mining, and fun-and-games at the YWCA summer camp all took their toll. In the 1960s, a well-meaning but ultimately ill-advised plan to corral the shifting sands from invading the conference grounds resulted in the planting of South African ice plant. This foreign invader drove out all the native vegetation.

I well remember attending a college student journalism conference at Asilomar way back when and tromping all over, around, and through the dunes late at night with a few cohorts and a bottle of cheap red wine. Kids! What did we know?

In 1984, **California State Parks** embarked on a project to restore the dunes, ripping out the ice plant, seeding native flora, and constructing a boardwalk so that visitors might still enjoy the dunes without tramping all over them. Thirty-five acres—all that remains of the original 480—have been returned to their more or less natural, pre-European state.

To begin this side trip, walk halfway around **The Circle**. At its farthest point from the social hall, turn toward the ocean onto the boardwalk.

A few yards west, make another right turn, still keeping on the boardwalk. The path will lead you on a serpentine stroll up a gentle to moderate incline. A free brochure from the information desk will introduce you to 23 native wildflowers that grow on this sandy, windswept spot at different times of the year, from Menzies' wallflower in February to mock heather signaling the start of autumn. The dunes also provide a home to bees, sparrows and hummingbirds, as well as the ever-present black-tail deer. If you wonder why some of the plants are enclosed in wire and mesh, it's to protect them from these inveterate floral and foliage munchers.

After the climb to the top of the dune, your reward is a nook of benches, ideal for watching the sunset. The boardwalk makes a fork at this point and the map on the **Asilomar Natural Dunes Preserve** brochure suggests you conclude this hike by taking the path to the right, leading back downhill on the boardwalk and ending at the chapel. An excellent choice in the dusky light post-sunset, or if you're dealing with a stroller or wheelchair.

As for me, I like the road less traveled, the leftward path at the fork. This short downhill walk ends at a pair of greenhouses, where the State Parks gardeners sprout the plants that will become parts of the dunes landscape. Next to the greenhouse is an outdoor swimming pool that always has me shivering a bit, trying to imagine plunging into the water at this usually foggy, chilly locale. I'm told, however, that the pool is heated and is actually quite comfortable.

From the pool, follow the brick pavers as they meander around a housekeeping building and **Parking Lot L**. A fenced-in, double padlocked, weed-choked area on the seaward side of the parking lot offers a puzzling scenario: an aging wooden hut, a couple of signs warning of FAA air traffic control, and a weird antenna or transmitting tower that looks to be of Cold War vintage. FAA air traffic control? In the middle of Asilomar, of all places? I've never been able to locate any answers, which only adds to its odd allure, like something out of a 1950s science fiction movie.

From the parking lot, head uphill on a fire road between **Spindrift North** and **Breakers West**. The sidewalk will then take you back to the chapel and from there to **Hearst Social Hall**, where our exploration of this "refuge-by-the-sea" comes to an end.

#7 WALKIN' THE GHOST RAILS

It will never die in the minds of those who knew it in its prime.

—Malcolm W. Steel, recalling a ride on the Del Monte Express in the early 1900s

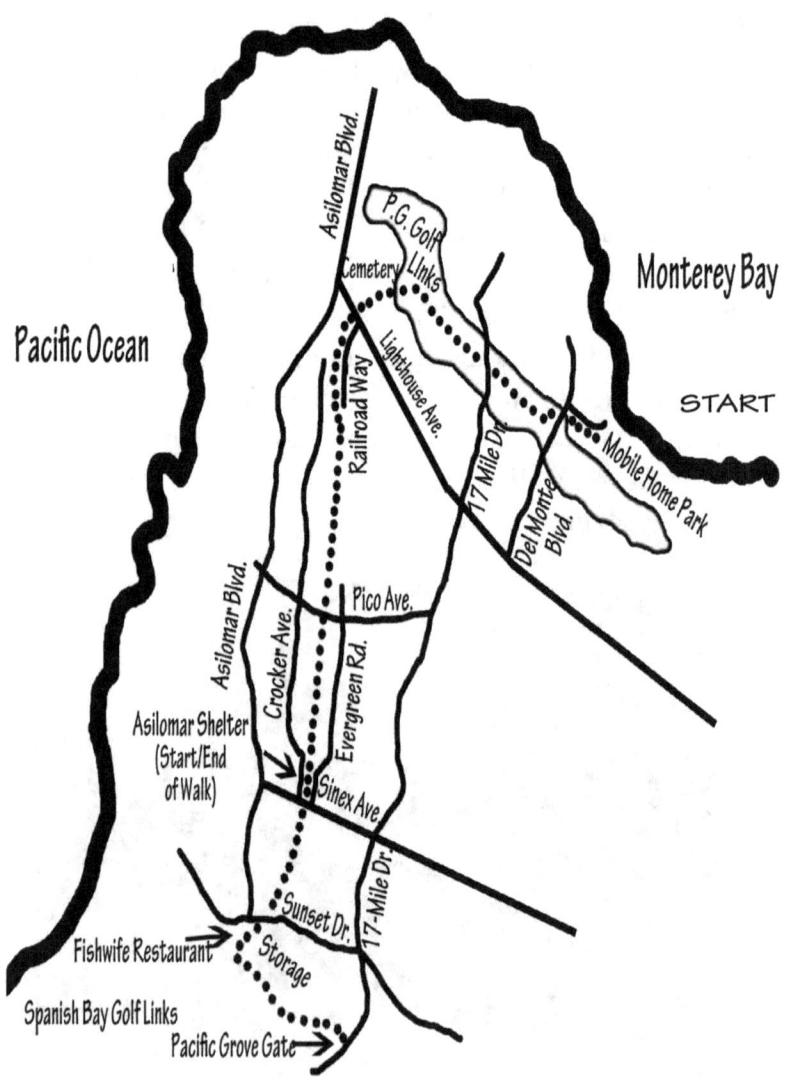

Old railroad bed that runs from the Pacific Grove Golf Links to Spanish Bay in Pebble Beach

- Roughly 2 miles one way, 4 miles round trip/±2500–8000 steps. In sections: Sinex Avenue to Pacific Grove Gate and back, 1-1/2 miles. Sinex Avenue to apartments at end of dirt path and back, 1-1/4 miles. Lighthouse Avenue to end of trail and back, 1-1/4 miles
- Surface: Dirt path, plus short stretch on pavement
- Public restrooms: At Asilomar Conference Grounds and on Spanish Bay Golf Links
- Parking: Free and unlimited on Sinex and Lighthouse avenues

In Brief: *When wind or fog make a walk on the shoreline bluffs unpleasant, the old* **Southern Pacific railbed** *offers an appealing alternative, steeped in local lore and featuring two very different golf courses.*

I like to tell people it was actually easier to get from the Bay Area to the Monterey peninsula 100 years ago than it is today, just to see their expressions of puzzlement and disbelief. It's true. A century ago, you could climb aboard a train, sit back and read the newspaper, knit, or even snooze, and a few leisurely hours later you'd find yourself disembarking at your vacation destination. Sure beats battling traffic on southbound Highway 101 on a busy summer weekend.

Rail service to Pacific Grove began in 1890 as an extension of the **Del Monte Express,** the passenger train that brought wealthy visitors from San Francisco to the posh **Hotel Del Monte** in Monterey, now the **Naval Postgraduate School.** The train ran through **Cannery Row** and hugged the edge of the bluffs to **Lovers Point.** The P.G. train station was located just beyond, where the Monarch Pines mobile home park now sits.

Long-time residents can be forgiven for wallowing in nostalgia as they share memories of the railroad days, for there truly are few things in life more evocative than a far-off train whistle, a sound not heard on the peninsula for 40-plus years. In the January 2004 issue of the **Pacific Grove Heritage Society's** *Board and Batten,* Elizabeth Haviside recalls the simple thrill of waiting at the station for the evening passengers to arrive. "We would get there early and watch the shoreline for the very first beam of the engine's headlight …. In the dusk of a summer evening, it seemed almost magical."

Keith Larson, in Book One of *Life in Pacific Grove,* says, "I still can picture playing at the main beach in the summers and waving to the engineer as the train approached the crossing at Ocean View Boulevard. The crossing at this street was the only one in town that had an electrified signal. So long, 'Friendly SP'."

Passenger train service continued on to the **YWCA camp at Asilomar** to meet seasonal demand on a route that cut through the front nine of the **Pacific Grove Golf Links**. The tracks then made a curving southward turn just before **El Carmelo Cemetery**, crossed Lighthouse Avenue, and continued on a line that ran between Crocker Avenue and Evergreen Road.

It all came to an end in 1971, when Amtrak took over the nation's passenger rail service. But freight trains continued to chug through Pacific Grove until 1979—more on that soon.

◘ ◘ ◘

We shall start this walk in the middle, as there is no place to leave a car at either end. Park anywhere on the city streets at the intersection of Sinex and Crocker avenues and make your way to a replica of the original **Asilomar passenger shelter,** located just north of the intersection. Its design was used throughout the Southern Pacific line for passenger shelters and is known as a **Greek cross**. Walls intersect 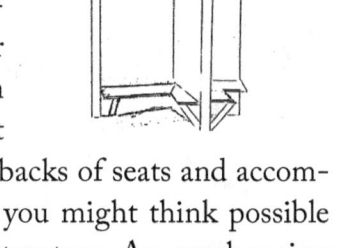 at 90 degree angles, forming the backs of seats and accommodating more passengers than you might think possible at first glance for such a small structure. An overhanging pyramid-shaped roof provided protection from rain, or in the case of Asilomar in the summertime, dense fog.

After admiring the craftsmanship and cleverness of design, turn to the south, crossing Sinex Avenue. As you pick up the dirt path, look to your feet. At the time of this writing, a few inches of what look to me like track are visible on the right side of the trail. Or perhaps that's my over-active imagination at work once again.

This section of old railbed on which we tread represents the last quarter mile or so of track that at one time serviced a **sand mining operation** at what is now the Spanish Bay resort in Pebble Beach. As we proceed along the trail, Hayward Lumber will be on your left, the **Asilomar Conference Grounds** to your right.

Use caution as you cross Sunset Drive, often busy with motor vehicle and bicycle traffic on weekends and during summer months. Once across Sunset, the path resumes between Pacific Grove Self-Storage and the Fishwife restaurant.

Back in the days when the freight trains still ran, the tracks split into two spurs at this point, both serving a sand mining operation at what was then known as **Lake Majella**. More of a pond than an actual lake, this was either a natural tidal swamp or a man-made byproduct of the sand mine. Or perhaps a combination of both. A fading mural on the side of German Motorwerks, 95 Central Avenue (best seen from the entrance to the next-door restaurant) depicting two Victorian ladies navigating a raft on Lake Majella lends credibility to the existence of a natural body of water before the sand mine arrived—unless it's purely the product of the muralist's imagination.

If you've ever walked barefoot on the beaches at Asilomar or Spanish Bay, you know the special qualities of our local sand, pure white and fine-grained. I'm fond of saying it's like walking through powdered sugar. Turns out, these tiny, high-grade quartz crystals are ideal for making glass. And thus was born the **Del Monte Sand Company**. The freight trains arrived in the afternoon, sometimes as many as 20 or 30 cars, to pick up sand that had already been washed, dried and bagged in the factory.

Keith Larson recalls "a spooky old sand plant, a collec-

tion of buildings which could be made even more mysterious by the incoming fog." Long-time Pagrovians have vivid memories of hearing the train's whistle, the clanking of the cars and the rumble of the engine as they toiled away in the classroom, perhaps daydreaming of the adventurous life riding the rails.

The nascent environmental movement of the 1970s saw growing demand to preserve what was left of the dunes, and the sand plant finally closed in 1978, ending the need for the railroad. Hayward Lumber was also a customer of the freight service, and the last train to run through Pacific Grove was actually making a delivery to the lumber yard in early 1979. Shortly afterward, the tracks were removed.

As our trail enters Pebble Beach, all traces of the original rail spurs, the sand factory, and Lake Majella are utterly and completely gone, the terrain dramatically altered with the construction of the Spanish Bay golf course, resort and condominiums in the 1980s. But the trail continues, no longer flat and straight to accommodate trains, but rather with gentle rises and declines. As the elevation increases, two very different sides of Pebble Beach come into view: the corp yard with all of its industrial equipment and warehouses to the left, and the manicured lawns of the **Spanish Bay Golf Links** to your right.

At the top of one rise, a small building offers what may be the nicest restroom facility on any public trail: heated, spotlessly clean and well-appointed. This restroom is obviously designed for use by the golfers who pay many hundreds of dollars to knock the ball around, not the likes of you and me, but as long as you slip in discreetly …

The trail ends a few additional uphill yards from the restroom at the **Pacific Grove Gate to Pebble Beach**. Turn around and return the way you came.

Once back at the **Asilomar passenger shelter**, we'll head north, on the flat, straight railroad bed. You may have noticed a weather-beaten For Sale sign on Sinex Avenue at the start of this portion of the trail. Technically, this right-of-way still belongs to Union Pacific, the successor to Southern Pacific. The California Coastal Commission has made it very clear the public has the right to use the trail and the railroad company cannot deny access by putting up fences or anything of that nature. The city maintains the trail by removing trees that have toppled during storms and filling muddy spots with wood chips.

I will have to 'fess up to a guilty pleasure along this portion of the trail: discreetly snooping into the backyards of the homes along Crocker and Evergreen, curious about the families that live there with their basketball courts, treehouses, and decks perfect for outdoor entertaining. Another cool feature is a concrete culvert stamped with its date of origin,1915, a reminder of the days when the train rolled along where we now walk.

The dirt path crosses Pico Avenue and continues along the narrow, tree-lined railbed until petering out at The Crest apartment complex. At this point, you may choose to turn around and finish the final leg of the walk on another day. To continue, walk for perhaps a quarter mile on pavement on the aptly named **Railroad Way** until you reach Lighthouse Avenue.

Use caution in crossing busy Lighthouse Avenue, then look for the trail to resume behind three wooden bollards to the left of the Lighthouse Lodge. The hotel will be on your right and the cemetery on your left. This is where the train tracks made the curve, back to the station at **Lovers Point** and then to points eastward.

Today, this curved portion of the trail is overgrown with shrubbery and at times is little more than a deer path. Once past the Lighthouse Lodge and Olympia West apartments, it becomes easier to follow, a straight shot right down the center of the front nine of the **Pacific Grove Golf Links**.

Known affectionately as "the poor man's Pebble," these original nine holes opened for play in 1932. The idea for a golf course on this site had been kicking around since 1929, the brainchild of **S.F.B. Morse**, whose **Del Monte Properties Company** owned the section of Pacific Grove known as the Beach Tract. He thought a golf course would make the land more attractive to potential development. Around the same time, the **P.G. Chamber of Commerce** was looking for ways to bring additional recreational facilities to the town. A deal was struck. In return for a gold coin worth $10, Morse would sell the land to the city with one condition—the city agreed to create and maintain the property as a golf course.

The railroad was already here, had been for nearly 40 years, and there's a part of me scratching my head over the idea of building a golf course with a train running right through it on a daily basis. Whose brilliant idea was that? It should be noted in fairness that the tracks never cut through any actual fairways or greens—the course was designed around the railroad right-of-way. At any rate, it seemed to work.

The old railbed runs right down the center of the course, a flat, straight path with wind-gnarled Monterey cypress on either side. Keep in mind that this is, indeed, a golf course and not everyone who plays it has the skill of Tiger Woods or Annika Sorenstam. Be aware of golfers in the vicinity, and as the saying goes, keep your eyes on the ball. I like to do this portion of the walk late in the day, when golf activity is not as intense as in the morning hours.

These days, a round of golf is no longer disturbed by the arrival of the SP freight train, but rather visitors of a much more quiet and benign nature. Our local deer seem completely oblivious to the balls flying overhead and the golf carts zipping around as they languidly munch the lush turf. For us hikers, it presents a tableau reminiscent of a British country estate: all that green, all those deer.

The trail crosses **17 Mile Drive** and then Del Monte Boulevard. Once across Del Monte, the path leaves the links, making a short dogleg to the left, and picks up atop a berm separating the golf course from the homes on Sea Palm Avenue. This short stretch is high enough that you'll be rewarded with a view of the blue waters of **Monterey Bay**.

The trail halts abruptly at a fence and a No Trespassing sign indicating the boundary of the mobile home park that replaced the railroad depot and with that, Pacific Grove's "romance of the rails" comes to an end.

EL CARMELO CEMETERY ENTRANCE

POINT PINOS LIGHTHOUSE ENTRANCE

#8 EL CARMELO CEMETERY AND POINT PINOS LIGHTHOUSE

Lighthouses don't go running all over an island looking for boats to save; they just stand there shining.
—Anne Lamott

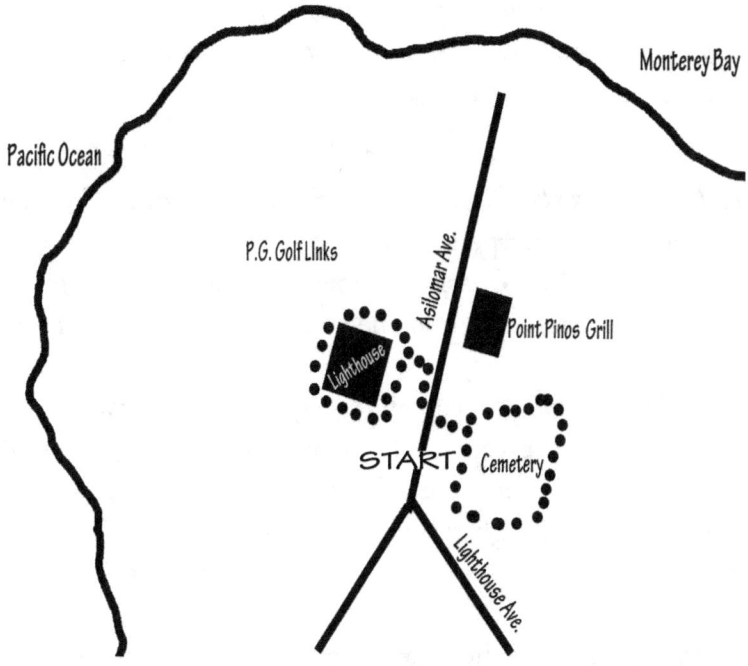

Loop through the cemetery and lighthouse grounds

- Roughly 1 mile/±2000 steps
- Surface: Pavement, asphalt mostly
- Public restrooms: Inside the Point Pinos Grill (clubhouse of the adjacent municipal golf course)
- Parking: Free and unlimited on lot on west side of Asilomar Boulevard

- No dogs permitted in either the cemetery or the lighthouse grounds
- Hours: Cemetery open daily dawn to dusk. Lighthouse open Thursday through Monday from 1:00 to 4:00 p.m. Closed Tuesdays and Wednesdays. Opens early on Saturdays at 10:00 a.m.

In Brief: *Lighthouses have traditionally served as symbols of safety and comfort, so it would seem a natural pairing—a walk through a cemetery, then a visit to a lighthouse.*

◘ ◘ ◘

To begin this stroll, set your GPS for 80 Asilomar Avenue and park in the perpendicular slots on the paved shoulder on the west side. Cross Asilomar Avenue (watching for traffic, of course) and enter the stone pillars of **El Carmelo Cemetery.**

A frolic through a cemetery may not be everyone's idea of a good time, except perhaps on Halloween, but burial grounds can offer a sense of profound serenity, as well as another peek through the telescope of history. El Carmelo feels especially restful with its tall cypress trees and scent of ocean air.

In addition to the dearly departed, El Carmelo provides a home for some very corporeal residents: *Odocoileus hemionus,* otherwise known as the black-tail deer. These hoofed ruminants are very common in Pacific Grove, and nowhere more than here in the cemetery. Perhaps I have a strange sense of humor, but I admit to finding it amusing to spot a deer lolling carefree as you please atop someone's gravesite, new life amidst all these reminders of the impermanence of it all.

Black-tail deer are found not just in Pacific Grove but all along the coast from Alaska to Baja California. As every avid gardener knows, these herbivores will eat just about anything: weeds, leaves, ornamental shrubs and pretty posies. Obviously, they love the well-tended lawn in the cemetery, not to mention the floral tributes left on the graves.

The Pacific Grove deer may seem tame, but they are wild animals and should be treated as such. Do not feed them, attempt to pet them, or venture too close for a photograph. They are basically peaceful and non-aggressive animals, but the doe will become protective and feisty if she has fawns bedded down nearby. *Dog walkers—be ever alert!*

El Carmelo Cemetery first appears on local maps in 1890 and has had a succession of owners over the years. In 1948, the city took over its care, clearing away the brush that had grown up over the oldest graves. Today, the city continues to sell traditional burial sites, as well as crypts and niches in the mausoleum and a special garden for urns. More information at https://www.cityofpacificgrove.org/living/el-carmelo-cemetery/cemetery-sites

We will start our stroll through the cemetery by bearing to the right on the asphalt road. It makes a wide arc, taking us to the oldest section with its upright granite headstones—some now tilting at odd angles—and simple wooden crosses. Many names associated with Pacific Grove's early years may be found here: **Berwick, Jewell, Dyke, Olmsted, Paul.**

One early figure is of particular interest to me as I live in the house that sports her plaque from the **Heritage Society—Lavinia Waterhouse**. She also happens to be the first person to be buried at El Carmelo. Mrs. Dr. Waterhouse, as she was known, spent most of her life in Sacramento where she made a living as a hydropathic physician and was a passionate campaigner for women's suffrage. She was also active in spiritualism and séances, brought about, no doubt, by the deaths of her husband and of seven of her ten children at young ages. Mrs. Dr. Waterhouse began spending her summers in Pacific Grove in 1882, investing heavily in real estate, passing away at age 81 in 1890.

For the longest time, given her dabbling in the paranormal, whenever anything odd would happen at home—flickering lights, slamming doors, odd gusts of wind—we'd always jokingly say, "There goes Lavinia." It was a bit disappointing, therefore, to discover from the Heritage Society that Mrs. Dr. Waterhouse never actually lived in my home. Instead it is the only one of the many properties she owned in Pacific Grove with the original house still standing. Because of her prominence in California in the late 1800s, the Heritage Society felt it appropriate to honor her with the plaque.

Other notables who have taken up permanent residence at El Carmelo:

Elizabeth Ann Steinbeck Ainsworth (1894-1992): sister of author John Steinbeck, outlived her famous brother by 32 years.

Eric Berne (1910-1970): Psychiatrist, founder of Transactional Analysis. His 1964 book *Games People Play* stayed on the best-seller list for weeks, eventually selling some five million copies.

John Cabell "Bunny" Breckenridge (1902-1996): Born in Paris, educated at Oxford, and heir to a large fortune in California (his family tree includes the founder of Wells Fargo), "Bunny" was flamboyantly gay in an era when it was not safe nor even legal to be so "out there." His lasting legacy is as an early pioneer for the gay community (*Bunny Breckenridge*, biography by Rod Woodard), and, alas, also for his one and only film role, as ruler of the aliens in Ed Woods's 1958 film, *Plan Nine from Outer Space*, considered by many critics to be the worst Hollywood movie ever made.

Claire Delmar (1901-1959): 1920s film actress who appeared in the first "talkie," *The Jazz Singer*. Her career, consisting of bit parts in silent and early sound films, is eclipsed by her violent death. On January 10, 1959, she was struck on the head outside her Carmel home, dragged inside, sexually assaulted and then stabbed to death with a steak knife. No killer was ever brought to justice and it remains an unsolved cold case.

The Reverend Sylvanus G. Gale and his wife **Jane Elizabeth (Cloyd) Gale**, early itinerant Methodist ministers to serve in Pacific Grove, 1890–1892. Rev. Gale built the first parsonage for the Methodist Church and both regularly attended Chautauqua meetings in Chautauqua Hall. Descendants continue to live in Pacific Grove.

Edward Edgar "Eddie" Lowery (1902-1984): Professional golf personality and member of the Caddy Hall of Fame. He is best known as the 10-year-old caddy of Francis Ouimet in the 1913 U.S. Open, considered "the greatest game ever played" by golf historians.

Continue on the circular roadway to the cannon marking the section of the cemetery devoted to veterans of the **Grand Army of the Republic** that served in the **U.S. Civil War**. Then onward, past the mausoleum with its crypts and niches for urns, and the outdoor urn garden, finally returning to the entrance.

An optional side trip involving a few extra yards of walking will take you to the Point Pinos Grill at 77

Asilomar Avenue. This is the clubhouse of the Pacific Grove Golf Links, and as a public building owned by the city, it's open to anyone. A moderately priced menu offers typical clubhouse fare—burgers, fish and chips, chowder—and there's a full bar. Restrooms are located to the left near the entrance. Open every day from roughly 7:00 to 7:00, closing an hour early on Sundays.

Back on our walking tour, cross Asilomar Avenue—once again, keeping your eye on traffic—and enter the grounds of the **Point Pinos Lighthouse**. Plan this portion of the walk during the hours that the lighthouse is open for visitation—

Thursday, Friday, Sunday and Monday, 1:00 to 4:00 p.m. and Saturdays from 10:00 a.m. to 4:00 p.m. Otherwise, you'll find a locked gate barring access, even if your intent is only to walk the grounds.

Point Pinos Lighthouse dates back to 1855 and is the oldest such facility in continuous operation on the West Coast. Though the days when ships regularly carried much-needed supplies to the communities of the Monterey peninsula are long past, the lighthouse remains in active operation as an aid to navigation under the jurisdiction of the **Coast Guard**. Its light blinks in a pattern of three seconds on, one second off, through a special lens invented by Frenchman **Augustin Fresnel**.

The lighthouse has had thirteen keepers from 1855 to 1964, two of them notable for being women. **Charlotte Layton** originally had the title of assistant to her husband, Charles, but when he was shot and killed while serving in a posse in 1855, she took over the job, becoming the first

female lighthouse keeper on the West Coast. Just imagine what it must have been like for this widow and her four children in this rugged, isolated spot, 15 years before the arrival of the Methodist summer encampment and with only a cart path through the forest connecting the lighthouse to the **pueblo of Monterey.** Mrs. Layton tended the light and raised her children in this place until 1860.

Another widow, **Emily Fish,** held the title of lighthouse keeper from 1893 to 1914, overseeing repairs after the 1906 earthquake damaged the lens and tower. It was Mrs. Fish who landscaped the grounds, evidence of her work visible today. She was popular in the community and loved to entertain, earning her the sobriquet of "the socialite keeper."

Since 1964, the Coast Guard has taken on the responsibility for upkeep of the lighthouse and in 2006 transferred full ownership of the property to the city. Today the **Heritage Society of Pacific Grove** and a cadre of dedicated volunteers maintain the building and grounds and make it available for public visits.

Admission is $5 for adults, $2 for kids age 7 to 17, and

free for age 6 and under. No charge to simply walk the grounds.

A group of antiques enthusiasts known as **Adobe Questers** helped furnish the lighthouse as it would have looked in the time of Emily Fish, who definitely believed in adding a feminine touch. Also inside you'll see artifacts such as the foghorn and a scale model of a device known as an eclipser, which allowed the light to blink at regular intervals in the days before electricity. As of this writing, the tower and lens has been off-limits as rusted panels in the lantern room are being restored.

The back nine of the **Pacific Grove Golf Links** surrounds the lighthouse on three sides. The original front nine, on the east side of Asilomar Avenue in back of the cemetery, has been around since 1932, but the links didn't become a full 18-hole golf course until 1960. Golf course architect **Jack Neville** had already worked on the design of the **Pebble Beach Golf Links** and the **Monterey Peninsula Country Club**'s shore course. He convinced the city to lease the property surrounding the lighthouse from the Coast Guard and pledged to design a course around the natural terrain of the dunes.

The back nine became Pacific Grove property in 2006 in the same agreement that deeded the lighthouse to the city. Today the links carry the nickname of "the poor man's Pebble," as its dramatic shoreline setting offers much of the same scenery and competitive challenges at a fraction of the cost of the courses in Pebble Beach.

Complete a circular stroll around the lighthouse and exit the grounds the same way you entered, having finished a leisurely walk offering, if you will, both the darkness of death and the hope and guidance of light.

#9 THE MONARCH BUTTERFLY SANCTUARY

Just like in fairy tales, you could stand in a clearing of the forest and butterflies would surround you, dancing in the sunlight.
—Rebecca Riddell

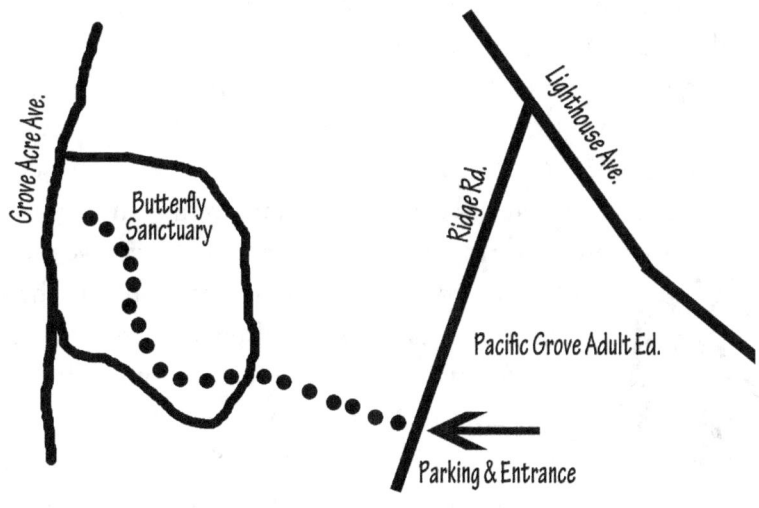

The Pacific Grove Monarch Butterfly Sanctuary, 250 Ridge Road

- 1/3 of a mile round trip/±667 steps
- Surface: Crushed granite, flat and with elevation changes
- Public restrooms: Unisex, ADA-compliant prefab toilet near the entrance
- Parking: Free and unlimited on Ridge Road on the side of the Pacific Grove Adult Education campus
- No dogs allowed

In Brief: *In a book about walks in* **Butterfly Town U.S.A.**, *of course we must include this easy stroll through the* **Monarch Butterfly Sanctuary**. *Best done between October and February, when our annual visitors are actually in town.*

Monarch butterflies (*Danaus plexippus*) have been spending their winters in Pacific Grove throughout its recorded history and undoubtedly far earlier. Old-timers will tell you of walking through town during winter months and being accompanied by literally clouds of black-and-orange flying insects, just like in the above quote by Rebecca Riddell in the first *Life in Pacific Grove.*

These little beauties cannot withstand temperatures that are either too cold or too hot. Thus, they leave their summer homes as far north as **Canada** when temperatures begin to drop and make their way to warmer climes, some winging their way all the way to **Mexico**. Their migration can cover up to 100 miles per day, reaching elevations as high as 10,000 feet. They tend to return to the same over-wintering spot every year, including Pacific Grove.

Now here's where it gets really amazing: the monarchs that arrive in the fall have *never* been here before! In fact, several generations have passed since the butterflies left the previous spring. How do these great-great-great grandchildren know exactly where they should return? It is one of those mysteries of nature for which science has no answer.

Sadly, the local monarch population has plummeted in recent years—an 85 percent crash from 2017 to 2018, 7,000 to 900 butterflies on the annual count. Similar drastic declines have been documented throughout the western states, with the usual suspects being fingered: habitat loss, pesticides, climate change.

What to do? As usual with these situations, there are no easy answers. It's difficult not to succumb to helpless despair as the fate of the very symbol of our town hangs in the balance. We were told to plant milkweed in our gardens, as it is the only plant on which monarchs can lay their eggs. Now we're told no, don't plant milkweed if you live near the coast, as it messes with their reproductive cycle. We were told to consider raising monarchs in captivity and releasing them. Now we're told no, don't do that—we may be introducing genetic mutations into the population. Some local residents—with the city's permission—are bringing in potted trees to augment the pines, eucalyptus and acacia growing naturally in the sanctuary in an attempt to entice more monarchs to stick around. Perhaps this will actually prove to be a good idea.

As for the rest of us, apparently what we *can* do is include nectar plants that provide food for monarchs in our gardens. Lay off the pesticides. And financially support organizations dedicated to helping the butterflies, like the Pacific Grove Natural History Museum.

To reach the sanctuary, watch for signs, one at the intersection of Lighthouse and Ridge Road, and another at the entrance. Park on Ridge Road next to the red buildings of the Pacific Grove Adult Education campus. A short walk, straight and flat, will lead you past the pink Butterfly Grove Inn and to the sanctuary itself. It is open dawn to dusk year 'round, with volunteer docents on duty most days between noon and 3:00 p.m. during the over-wintering months. Closed during times of high wind due to danger of falling tree branches. Free admission; donations appreciated.

◘ ◘ ◘

At the entrance, you'll be greeted by a large plywood butterfly, perfect for photographs. Then simply follow the leisurely winding path through the trees until it ends at Grove Acre Road. Signs along the path provide an instant education on monarchs, their habitat and their migration.

To see those much-photographed clusters of monarchs, plan to arrive as early in the morning as you can, before they fly off for the day in search of nectar. Simply look up into the trees. What may at first appear to be a bunch of dead leaves is probably a cluster of butterflies. Binoculars are most helpful.

Be sure to stick to the path—no one wants to accidentally step on a butterfly! Don't try to touch them or pick them up. Pacific Grove has a law forbidding "molestation of butterflies" and it carries a $1,000 fine.

Other ways to "get your butterfly on" in Pacific Grove:

Museum of Natural History: Includes a permanent monarch gallery and gift shop that sells nectar plant seeds and butterfly-themed merchandise. Located at 165 Forest Avenue (corner of Forest and Central) and open daily from 10:00 a.m. to 5:00 p.m. Admission $8.95 for adults, $5.95 for youth, students and military. Free for Monterey County residents.

Butterfly Days: Usually the first Friday, Saturday and Sunday in October, this community festival celebrates the return of the monarchs. The events vary from year-to-year, often including a bazaar, historic walking tours, art exhibits, and live entertainment. One tradition has remained sacrosanct for 80-plus years: the Saturday morning parade in the downtown district featuring costumed children from local schools. The kindergarteners dressed as monarchs with their black-and-orange construction paper wings and bobbing antennae are simply too precious! If you cannot make it to the parade, you can get a taste of the utter cuteness of it all by visiting the **Butterfly Children statue** in front of the U.S. Post Office, 680 Lighthouse Avenue.

Butterfly House: This private residence at 309 Ninth Street is an explosion of color, like something out of the Beatles' *Yellow Submarine*, turning an otherwise ordinary house into a work of folk art. There's a poignant story behind all this whimsy. Homeowner J Jackson's wife, Sonja, was losing her eyesight but could still see bright colors. So he transformed their home into a canvas of wild, vibrant color with butterflies galore—a true labor of love. Please keep in mind that this is a private home. If you must take a picture—and of course you must—be kind and stay on the sidewalk.

#10 GEORGE WASHINGTON PARK

This is the forest primeval.
—Henry Wadsworth Longfellow

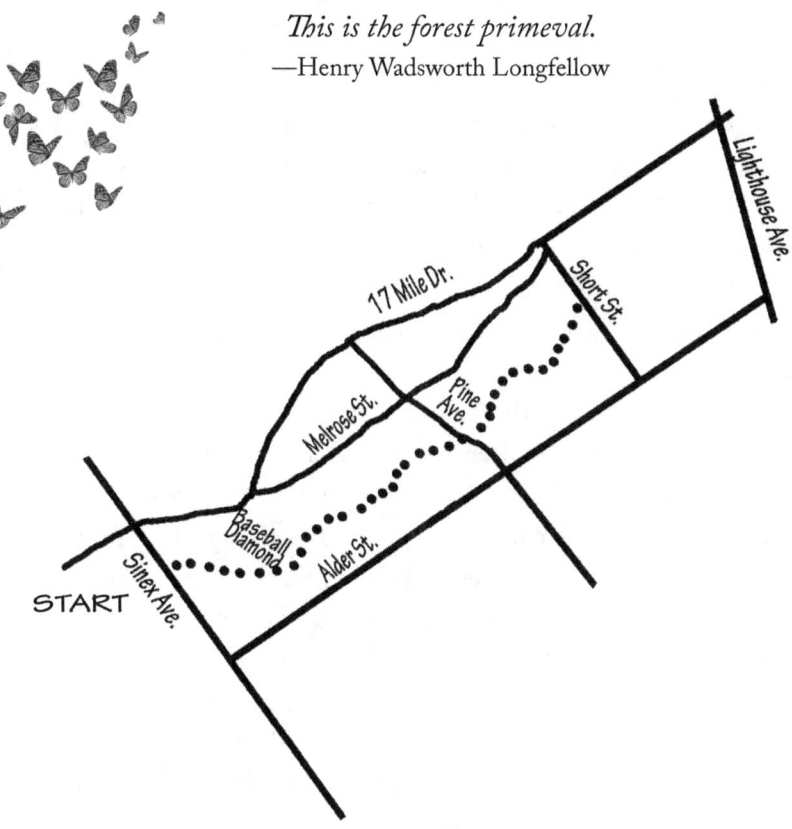

Sinex Avenue to Short Street

- 1/2 mile one way, 1 mile round trip/±1000–2000 steps
- Surface: Dirt path
- Public restrooms: At the Sinex Avenue side of the park
- Parking: Free and unlimited on surrounding streets
- Dogs allowed off-leash before 9:00 a.m. or after 4:00 p.m.

In Brief: *An easy walk through a woodsy oasis in the middle of the city, and with an intriguing backstory—that's George Washington Park.*

A first-time visitor to this city park could be forgiven for assuming this dense thicket of Monterey pine and oaks has stood here since the beginning of time, like something out of Longfellow's prelude to *Evangeline:* This is the forest primeval. "The murmuring pines ... bearded with moss, and in garments green, indistinct in the twilight, stand like Druids of eld ...."

Understandable. But wrong.

Russell Sunshine offers a detailed origin story of George Washington Park, based on extensive historical research, in the first edition of *Life in Pacific Grove*. The fact is, by the mid-19th century, the forest was essentially gone, cleared—mostly by burning—to make way for cattle grazing. This activity had ended by the turn of the 20th century and new trees began to shoot up on the barren and abandoned expanse of land. For summer visitors who didn't want to subject themselves to the strict regulations of the **Methodist Retreat** (no booze, no dancing, no gambling, no fun!), it became the ideal spot to pitch a tent.

In 1926, the city of Pacific Grove purchased the land from the **Del Monte Properties Company**. It officially received the name of our nation's first president in 1932, in a ceremony featuring a brass band, speeches by leaders of the local **American Legion post**, and a flag-raising ceremony.

What followed was a decades-long debate over the best use of these 12 city blocks of open space.

Remember those campers who first showed up during the Methodist era? Much like the annual migration of the monarch butterflies, those vacationers continued to return summer after summer to camp out at the southern end of the park. During **World War II**, the city even began to allow trailers as well as tents. Someone had the idea in 1948 of boosting city revenues by adding cement parking pads and sewer hook-ups. This galvanized the neighbors into action, pushing through an ordinance prohibiting all camping—trailer and tent—in the park.

You'd think this would signal the end of any talk of development for this small forest, preserving it forever. You would be wrong.

In 1960, the mayor of Pacific Grove had a brilliant idea—let's appropriate all of the park south of Pine Avenue for a new civic center. Just picture city hall, the police department and the fire station in a mid-century modern government complex on Sinex Avenue on the western edge of our little town. This time, **Mrs. W.R. Holman**—yes, *that* Holman, as in the department store—came to the rescue. She argued, quite logically, that this property represented the last "grove" in Pacific Grove, and a crowd of irate citizens agreed with her. The plans for the new civic center were quietly laid to rest.

◘ ◘ ◘

We'll begin our ramble through George Washington Park at its southern edge, Sinex Avenue. Look for the path at roughly the halfway point between Alder Street and **17 Mile Drive**.

At first impression, the image is one of a typical suburban municipal park with the usual tot playground, picnic tables, barbecue grills, and cinderblock restroom building. Where, you may rightly wonder, is the promised wooded sanctuary?

Patience. It's coming.

Continue on the path through the picnic area with the playground to your left. A gentle incline will take you to a baseball diamond. Two benches overlook the outfield—Pacific Grove's version of the bleacher seats.

Stay to the right, down a slight decline, when the trail forks. Just like that, the urban world falls away and you find yourself in an enchanted forest. It's especially magical in the spring, when the grasses that carpet the forest floor are green and tiny white and yellow wildflower blossoms peek through. Wind-gnarled trees dripping with lichen add to the wild, remote atmosphere, the silence broken only by the sounds of chattering birds and squirrels ... and your own footsteps crunching on the path.

On my first visit, I found myself peering from time-to-time to the right, through the dense curtain of leaves, pine needles and lichen and around tree trunks to catch a glimpse of the homes on Alder Street, just to reassure myself that I really was still in Pacific Grove and not in some far-off wilderness. The effect really is that profound.

One Yelp reviewer wrote, "The simplicity of the park is its greatest beauty." I could not agree more.

There is a price to pay for all of this natural beauty: George Washington Park is one of the few places in Pacific Grove where poison oak is likely to grow. Stay on the path and avoid brushing against plants with leaves in clusters of three. If you think your pooch has frolicked in a patch of the stuff, best to wash him thoroughly when you arrive home.

As our woodsy stroll continues, we'll be momentarily thrust back into civilization when we reach Pine Avenue. Watch for cars, natch, before you cross. The trail picks up on the far side of the street, with more delightful steps through this serene sanctuary. If you want to pretend that these oaks and pines are ancient relics of a much earlier time, just like Longfellow's "forest primeval," that's okay. Historic fact notwithstanding, it's hard not to shake that first impression.

The park and this walk come to an end all too soon as we reach Short Street. At this point, turn around and retrace your steps to Sinex on the same path, or make two right turns, returning on Alder Street to the starting point with **The Last Hometown** on one side and an ancient forest—or at least, the appearance of one—on the other.

#11 LYNN "RIP" VAN WINKLE OPEN SPACE

You think dogs will not be in heaven? I tell you, they will be there long before any of us.
—Robert Louis Stevenson

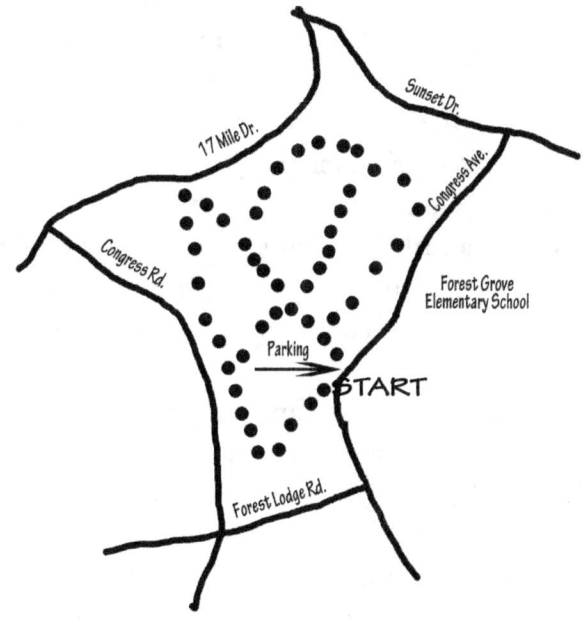

Loop or "there and back" trail between Congress Avenue and 17 Mile Drive

- Roughly 1 to 1.2 miles/±2000–2400 steps
- Surface: Dirt path
- Public restrooms: None
- Parking: Free and unlimited at turnout on Congress Avenue
- Dogs allowed off-leash before 9:00 a.m. or after 4:00 p.m.

In Brief: *Locals refer to this as "the dog park" and that says it all!*

For the longest time, I puzzled over the name of this park. Rip Van Winkle? What does Pacific Grove have to do with Washington Irving's tale of a henpecked husband who falls asleep for 20 years after playing a game of nine-pins and drinking alcoholic beverages with a bunch of mysterious men in the mountains? I mean, we're a long way from the Catskills.

Little did I know, our park has nothing to do with the creator of the Knickerbocker tales of the Dutch settlers of New Amsterdam, other than similarities of the name. Instead, it honors a real, 20th century person, Lynn "Rip" Van Winkle, a local resident who campaigned tirelessly to have these 20 acres of Monterey pine forest preserved as open space.

With a last name like Van Winkle, it was inevitable that young Lynn would earn the lifetime nickname of "Rip." Born in 1936 in Montana, he grew up near Yellowstone National Park, where he developed a deep passion for wilderness and the natural world. He became a public school educator and moved to Pacific Grove in 1967 with his wife Judy, also a teacher.

Van Winkle threw himself into outdoorsy pursuits, joining the **Sierra Club** and volunteering with **Scouting**. In 1972, he was an active campaigner for Proposition 20, which created the **California Coastal Commission**.

Like many other communities in California, the 1950s through the early 1970s saw a growth boom in Pacific Grove. The Del Monte Park subdivision sprang up, as well as the Forest Hill shopping district. Dismayed at this rapid loss of open space, Van Winkle led the charge to save this large swath of undeveloped forest land. At the time, the acreage was owned by Del Monte Properties, predecessor of the Pebble Beach Company. The forest was surrounded by fences, with just a few small pass-throughs so children who lived in Pebble Beach could walk to Forest Grove Elementary and P.G. High.

Members of the PGHS cross-country track team used the forest for their practice runs, so they eagerly joined the crusade to save the land from potential development. Even though they were too young to vote, they went door-to-door to distribute literature in favor of a $100,000 bond measure to purchase the property. The voters approved the bond issue in 1974. The fences came down and what was then known as **Forest Grove Open Space** was on its way.

Tragedy struck in 1979, when Van Winkle succumbed to cancer when he was only 43 years old. A grateful City Council voted to rename the park in honor of the man whose vision and energy made it possible: Lynn "Rip" Van Winkle.

Today, the open space is overseen jointly by the city of Pacific Grove and the **Monterey Peninsula Regional Park District** and is left pretty much in its wild, untouched state with minimal interference from the so-called civilized world—except, of course, the dogs.

◘ ◘ ◘

To start our hike, drive southwest on Congress Avenue after crossing Sunset Drive from the central part of town. On your left, you'll first see the **Pacific Grove High School** football field, and then **Forest Grove Elementary School**. Just past the elementary school, look for a turnout on your right that accommodates perhaps six or eight cars. Park here.

In a town that is overall very dog-friendly, this place

is the epicenter of all things canine, thanks to the off-leash tradition and the acres of woodsy delights to sniff, lift a leg against, and romp through. Your first hint of the special nature of this park is the sign board a few feet from the turnout, featuring flyers promoting dog grooming services, pet-sitters, and lost-and-found of the furry, four-legged variety. On one of my visits, a fellow who had written a book with a dog-related theme had left a stack of bookmarks—now, that's marketing to your target audience!

If you do allow your dog to run off-leash, he should be under your voice command, and should be friendly, or at least nonaggressive, when it comes to meeting strangers of both the human and canine variety. Mostly, the dogs that frequent Rip Van Winkle delight in the chance to play around with members of their own species, but there have been a few unfortunate incidents.

And the saying goes—if your pooch poops, you will be a good citizen and clean it up.

Rip Van Winkle Open Space represents the only hike in Pacific Grove where a person could conceivably get lost. Rather than one central trail, it consists of a network of meandering paths with no clear markings or directional signs. If you keep bearing to the right, you will end up making a loop around the park. Or, stick to the widest path, heading downhill through the middle of the park until you reach **17 Mile Drive**, then turn around and retrace your steps. You could keep going, eventually arriving at **Spanish Bay**, but this is a book about Pacific Grove hikes, not Pebble Beach, so we'll stop here.

I don't think you *really* could get lost. One dog-walker describes it as "getting lost in a shopping mall"—in other words, confusing at first, but essentially a finite space surrounded by roads. If you do become disoriented, remember that if you keep heading uphill, you will eventually return to Congress Avenue. From there, it's easy enough to walk on the shoulder back to your vehicle.

A greater danger is posed by the presence of poison oak. Stay on the trail, and avoid brushing up against any bush or vine with pointed leaves in clusters of three. Rinse off Fido when you arrive home if you think there's a chance he came in contact with the nasty stuff.

As Pacific Grove's largest expanse of undeveloped terrain, this park is home to creatures like foxes, raccoons, possums, and deer, though the presence of dogs in the daylight hours will send them scurrying into their burrows and thickets until twilight and dawn. More than likely, the only critters you'll encounter during your hike will be birds, squirrels and of course—dogs, dogs, and more dogs.

#12 HISTORIC DOWNTOWN PACIFIC GROVE

It was just beautiful, that's all.

—W.R. Holman, describing his first impressions of Pacific Grove when he arrived in 1888

Guide to Numbers on the Map

1. Holman Building
2. Pacific Grove Art Center
3. Bank of Pacific Grove
4. Winston Hotel
5. Site of Methodist Church
6. Post Office
7. Digital Research, Inc.
8. Octagon Replica
9. Hart Mansion
10. Gosby House
11. Reincarnation Vintage Clothing
12. Ketcham's Barn
13. City Hall
14. Grove Market
15. Chinese Wedding Mural
16. Victorian Commercial Block
17. St. Mary's-by-the-Sea
18. Pacific Grove Public Library
19. Jewell Park
20. Chautauqua Hall
21. Elmarie Dyke Open Space
22. Centrella Inn
23. Victorian Cottages
24. Museum of Natural History

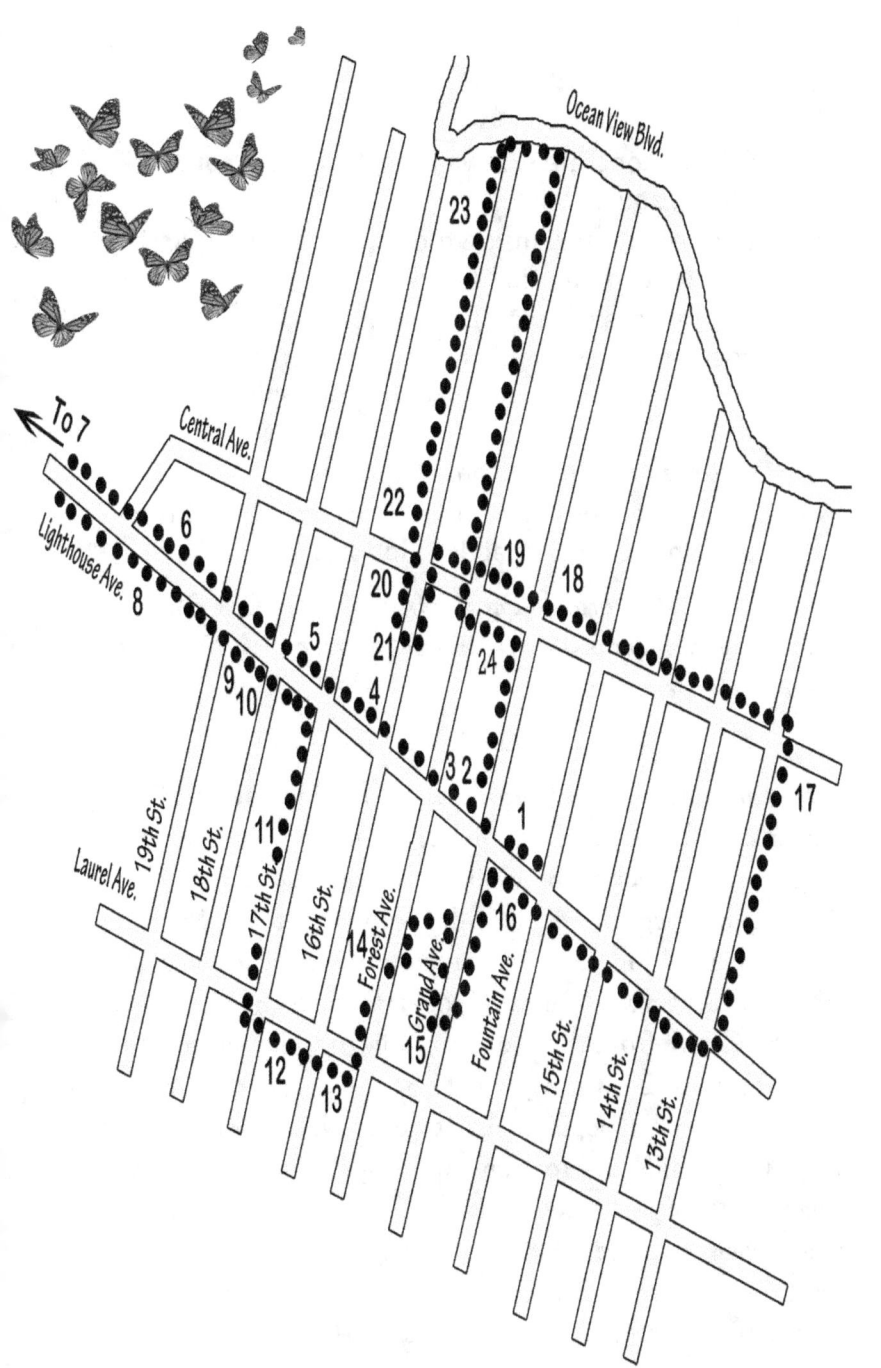

Downtown Pacific Grove

- Two mile loop/±4000 steps
- Surface: Concrete sidewalk, asphalt road, some inclines, some stairs
- Public restrooms: Inside the Library, Natural History Museum and City Hall
- Parking: Free but with limits (mostly two hours) on streets in the commercial district. Read the signs! Free and unlimited on surrounding residential streets.
- Dogs may not be welcome in all buildings
- Some attractions have limited hours and will be so noted in the individual descriptions.

In Brief: *A stroll through Pacific Grove's downtown district offers a panorama of history from pre-historic eras to the dawn of the digital age.*

◘ ◘ ◘

Start our downtown historic tour at the **Holman Building**, covering the entire city block on the northern side of Lighthouse Avenue between Fountain and Grand. From its humble beginnings as a dry goods store in 1891 into a commercial juggernaut during the first seven decades of the 20th century, **Holman's Department Store** simply *was* Pacific Grove from the moment of its grand opening at this location in 1924. Immortalized in *Cannery Row* and for a time the largest department store between San Francisco and Los Angeles, Holman's was much more than just a place to shop. It played a key role in the 1958 revival of the **Feast of Lanterns** and hosted generations of delighted children on the **Santa Claus Express**, a holiday train that ran between the Monterey and Pacific Grove stations.

The store's owner and president, **William Rensselaer Holman**, died in 1981 and in 1984, the store was sold to a regional chain called **Ford's**. It might have remained a department store under this new name had the Loma Prieta earthquake not struck in 1989. The Pacific Grove store came through relatively unscathed, but the big shaker leveled the Ford's stores in Watsonville and Santa Cruz. The company declared bankruptcy and shuttered all of its properties. An antique mall occupied the first floor of the Holman's building for the next couple of decades. Today, as the old warhorse nears its centennial, it's seeing new life as luxury condominiums, a repurposing that Mr. Holman most likely could never have imagined, but hopefully would have approved of.

Proceed west on Lighthouse Avenue, crossing Grand Avenue, to the awning at the stairway leading to the **Pacific Grove Art Center** on the second floor. This nonprofit offers four rooms of exhibit space, classes for adults and children, and studios available for rent. The Art Center opened in 1969 during those trippy days when Pacific Grove boasted the largest concentration of hippies between San Francisco and Los Angeles. 1969 was also the year that Pacific Grove dropped its ban on booze (the last dry town in the state) and legend has it that the first legal alcoholic drink to be served in P.G. was at the July 4 grand opening of the Art Center.

Open Wednesdays through Saturdays, 12:00 to 5:00 p.m.; Sundays from 12:00 to 4:00 p.m. Free admission.

Continuing west on Lighthouse, we next encounter  the **Bank of Pacific Grove** at the corner of Lighthouse and Forest, now a real estate office. Built in 1904, it appears to be constructed of heavy granite blocks, but the material is actually a siding meant to simulate stone. It's said to be the only example of **Romanesque revival architecture** on the Monterey Peninsula.

The blue building at the northwest corner of 16th and Lighthouse is little changed since its origins as the **Winston Hotel** in 1904. Architectural historians believe it is the first building in Pacific Grove to be constructed in the **Mission Revival style** and the first to be covered with stucco.

Proceed west on Lighthouse Avenue to the block bordered between 17th and 18th streets. This 1960s-era complex of shops, offices and the International Cuisine restaurant is the **site of the original Methodist church**, built in 1883 by the founders of our town. During the early years, the lighted cross atop the tallest spire of this Gothic structure shone so brightly, it was used by ships as a navigational aid. As the decades wore on and church membership dwindled, the grand old building was simply too difficult to maintain. It was demolished in 1963 and the congregation moved to a new, modern-style church on Sunset Drive.

As we continue west on Lighthouse Avenue, pause to admire the massive eucalyptus tree spilling out onto the sidewalk in front of the **Post Office**, one of many such trees in Pacific Grove that started out as seeds from Australia planted in 1880 by a Methodist bishop.

I know these aromatic trees have gotten a bad rap in recent years as an invasive, non-native species and all that, but I still love the aroma of eucalyptus in the damp, salt air.

While we're at the Post Office, take a peek inside at the mural depicting an idyllic summer day at **Lovers Point**, created in 1940 by way of a Depression-era federal program known as the **Treasury Section of Fine Arts**. The artist, Victor Arnautoff, was all but forgotten until a firestorm of public controversy erupted in 2019 over a mural he created way back in 1936 for George Washington High School in San Francisco. As of this writing, it's unclear what will happen—the offending images of slaves and Native Americans painted over, hidden behind curtains, or something else entirely? Time will tell.

As we leave the Post Office, be sure to say hello to the charming **Butterfly Children statue**, created in 1996 by **Christopher Bell**, the local sculptor we met on the Rec Trail East walk.

Continue west on Lighthouse Avenue for some five city blocks. Cross Lighthouse when you reach Pacific Avenue, then walk west one block, crossing Willow Street. The Victorian home at the southwest corner functioned in the 1970s as the Pacific Grove equivalent of a Silicon Valley garage, a workshop where digital history was forged. **Gary**

Kildall and his wife **Dorothy** founded **Digital Research, Inc.**, which created a program called CP/M (Control Program for Microcomputers). CP/M allowed a microprocessor to communicate for the first time with a disk drive storage unit. Got that?

In 2014, the **Institute of Electrical and Electronic Engineering** placed a plaque in the sidewalk on the Willow Street side of this corner lot. It notes that the achievements that took place inside this private home "provided an important foundation for the personal computer revolution."

As to what happened to Gary Kildall and his company, and why PCs now run on Bill Gates' MS-DOS instead of Gary Kildall's CP/M—and more to the point, why Pacific Grove never began "Silicon Grove"—check out the article by David A. Laws in Book One of *Life in Pacific Grove*.

Turn around and make your way back to the downtown business district on the south side of Lighthouse Avenue. The odd-shaped little structure at the intersection with Park Avenue in front of BookWorks is not historic, but it gives us a glimpse at two Pacific Grove buildings that definitely would be considered significant, if only they still existed. **The octagon** was an architectural fad that made its way to the West Coast in the late 1800s. The theory held that a circle was the ideal shape for a building when it came to making maximum use of space and light. With construction in a true circular fashion difficult-to-impossible to carry out, an eight-sided shape was considered the next best thing. The original **Natural History Museum** and the first **Board of Trade**, forerunner to the **Chamber of Commerce**, were both built as octagons and both occupied space in and around Jewell Park. Neither lasted into the 21st century, or even all that long into the 20th, but the little structure at Bookworks gives us an idea of what they looked like.

At 649 Lighthouse Avenue is a stunning example of one of our town's iconic Victorians, the **Hart Mansion.** Built in 1893 by a physician, **Dr. Andrew Jackson Hart**, you can still see  his name immortalized in stained glass above the front door. For some 70 years, this home remained in the Hart family. From the 1970s onward, a succession of restaurants have occupied the Hart Mansion, the latest being an ice cream shop called Cream and Crumbles. As of this writing, the hours were somewhat limited, basically Fridays, Saturdays and Sundays in the afternoon and evening.

The Gosby House, on the same block at 643 Lighthouse Avenue, is one of the Victorian bed-and-breakfast inns for which Pacific Grove is sought after by  honeymooners and couples celebrating anniversaries. It was constructed in 1888 by **J.S. Gosby**, the owner of Pacific Grove's first shoe store. From the beginning, Gosby accepted boarders into his home, functioning pretty much the same as today's B&B—although perhaps not offering the late afternoon wine and hors d'oeuvres spread.

Continue east on Lighthouse Avenue for one block and make a right turn onto 17th Street. The west side is lined with charming cottages from the 1880s to the early 1900s, now converted to commercial uses. Of particular interest is **Reincarnation Vintage Clothing** at 217, a used clothing store that's been around since the hippie-dippy days of the 1970s. Open daily except Sunday from 11:00 a.m. to 6:00 p.m.

Turn left on Laurel Avenue and cross the street to find **Ketcham's Barn**, the headquarters of the **Pacific Grove Heritage Society**. This is the organization that places those green plaques on the front of older homes throughout town with the name of the original owner and the year of construction. Many visitors and residents alike are curious as to why so many homes bear the names of women during an

era when "the fair sex" was not even allowed to vote. No one seems to know for sure, though it's speculated some of these women may have been widows, while others may have been listed by their husbands as the owner on the tax rolls to protect the family home should his business fail. Hello? Did I hear someone say "taxation without representation"?

Ketcham's Barn was built in 1891 by **H.C. Ketcham** for the purpose, as you might guess, of housing animals, their feed and equipment. The city purchased the by-then derelict property in 1979 and leased it to the Heritage Society, which uses it to house a hodgepodge of artifacts and curios from Pacific Grove's Victorian era. Open Saturdays from 1:00 to 4:00 p.m., free admission.

One block east on Laurel, at the intersection with Forest Avenue, is **Pacific Grove City Hall**. Although incorporated as a city in 1889, the town did not get an official seat of government until one was constructed on this site in 1912. Many of its original design elements, best described as eclectic, are still

evident. The clock tower, from which bells ring out every quarter hour and can be heard throughout the downtown district, was originally built for hanging fire hoses to dry. City Hall was substantially renovated and expanded in 2001, including the addition of public restrooms accessible from the courtyard on Laurel Street. City Hall is open Monday through Friday from 8:00 a.m. to noon and 1:00 to 5:00 p.m.

A half-block walk downhill on Forest, toward the bay, takes you to a beloved Pacific Grove institution: the **Grove Market**. When Charlie Higuera opened the doors for business in 1969, it was

one of seven small, independent grocery stores in Pacific Grove. Now, it's the only one left. I am always amazed at the variety of food stuffs, household staples, and handy items ranging from playing cards to first aid adhesive tape packed into 5,000 square feet. Curious about the unusual shape of the building? Before it was the Grove Market, this building was part of a mid-century supermarket chain that used an oversized Quonset hut as an attention-getting design element. The Grove Market is open daily from 8:00 a.m. to 7.00 p.m., closing at 6;00 p.m. on Sundays.

Before leaving the Grove Market, check out the mural on the northern side of the building by Pacific Grove painter Jerry Boyajian showing the progression of the stuff we eat from the farm to a picnic by the sea.

Cross Forest Avenue, make your way downhill, then turn right into the parking lot between Max's Grill and Chase Bank. Emerge on Grand Avenue, turn right, and walk a few yards uphill to the **Chinese Wedding Mural** on the side of Pacific Grove Cleaners. Created in 2009 by **Merlin Brown**, the mural commemorates the 1900 wedding of an early member of the Chinese community, known only as **Jim-Jim**, who ran the town's first laundry. The traditional festivities featured lighted paper lanterns, quite possibly the inspiration for the town's Victorian ladies to create the **Feast of Lanterns**.

Turn around and head downhill to Lighthouse Avenue. Cross Grand Avenue, walking east, to the **Victorian**

commercial block. These colorfully painted and richly detailed retail shops and restaurants are authentic and date to the 1800s. The location of the current trio of Marita's boutiques started out as a pharmacy owned by **C.K. Tuttle**, whose lasting legacy was not so much the dispensing of medicine, but the expansive photographic record he created of our town's early years. His daughter, **Winnifred Tuttle**, was Pacific Grove's first telephone operator, working on a switchboard in her father's drugstore.

Continue your stroll east on Lighthouse Avenue to 13th Street. Cross Lighthouse in front of another massive example of the eucalyptus trees planted by that early Methodist bishop. Walk down 13th Street, heading toward the bay, passing by the home with the **Heritage Society** plaque for **Lavinia Waterhouse**, whom we met on walk #8- El Carmelo Cemetery and Point Pinos Lighthouse.

You may be surprised to learn—I know I was—that the oldest church in Pacific Grove was *not* constructed by the Methodists. The proof is the deep red Gothic structure at the corner of Central Avenue and 13th Streets. **St. Mary's-by-the-Sea** is an Episcopal church, built in 1887 with a design copied from a church in Bath, England. Its distinctive features include two Tiffany windows donated by **Cyrus McCormick**, nephew of the inventor of the mechanical reaper, who was married here in 1889.

Cross Central Avenue and head west, covering three blocks until you reach the **Pacific Grove Public Library**. This irreplaceable community resource saw its beginnings in 1886 as a "reading corner" in a community hall known as the **Old Parlor** at the corner of what is now Fountain Avenue and Ricketts Row. In 1904, the city's avid readers received a double windfall: a Carnegie grant of $10,000 and the dona-

tion of land by the **Pacific Improvement Company**, making a real library possible. The library opened on this site in 1908.

Over the decades, various expansion and modernization schemes resulted in the near-disappearance of the original **Carnegie Mission Revival-style architecture**. As of this writing, the library is in the early stages of an ambitious renewal project to both reveal and restore the original design elements while upgrading facilities and fixtures and just basically bringing the library into the 21st century. Hours: Monday-Tuesday-Wednesday, 12:00 to 7:00 p.m.; Thursday, 10:00 a.m. to 7:00 p.m.; Friday, 12:00 to 5:00 p.m.; Saturday, 10:00 a.m. to 5:00 p.m. Closed Sundays. During renovation the library has set up quarters in the Holman building.

Continue west on Central Avenue, crossing Grand Avenue, to reach **Jewell Park**. This was the site of the original open-air temple of the **Methodist Retreat**, and is named for **Dr. F.F. Jewell**, the first Pacific Grove Methodist minister. The temple consisted of a stage and benches, arranged in an octagonal shape. If you've ever wondered why Central Avenue makes a slight jog at Jewell Park, now you know— to make way for the odd design of the Methodists' open-air temple.

For many years, a large, ornate Victorian fountain dominated Jewell Park, donated by **Dr. Henry Daniel Cogswell**, a 19th century dentist and temperance crusader. He was convinced that if people had access to safe, cool drinking water, they wouldn't turn so readily to alcoholic beverages. Thus, he paid for the installation of public water fountains in cities and towns throughout the nation. One might wonder why Dr. Cogswell thought Pacific Grove might be in need of such an amenity, given the Methodists' unyielding ban on booze, but it's one of those little mysteries lost to history. At any rate, Dr. Cogswell's fountain remained in Jewell Park until 1942, when it made the ultimate patriotic sacrifice to a **World War II** scrap metal drive.

Today Jewell Park features a charming gazebo in the Victorian style and a small building known appropriately enough as the **Little House**. Built and donated to the city by the Pacific Grove Rotary in 1952, it hosts a variety of community functions and events, everything from A.A. meetings to one-man theatrical performances.

One block west of Jewell Park, on the opposite side of the street, is a barn-like structure known as **Chautauqua Hall**. Another relic of the Methodist Retreat, it was built in 1881 to provide a venue for concerts, lectures, and other "moral attractions," and also to store tents during the off-season. The name comes from an adult education movement known as the **Chautauqua Literary and Scientific Circle** that swept the nation in the late Victorian era and had its beginnings at Lake Chautauqua in New York. In

the early days, Chautauqua lectures took place either in this building or in the tent in Jewell Park. The scientific presentations would often focus on marine biology—a precursor, perhaps, of **Hopkins Marine Station** and the **Monterey Bay Aquarium**. Chautauqua Hall became a **California Historic Landmark** in 1970. Today, it's available to rent for wedding receptions and the like and is home to the DiFranco Dance Project, a Friday night freestyle dance jam, and Jazzercise—activities that surely would have raised an eyebrow or two among our town's straightlaced ancestors.

In back of Chautauqua Hall is a small park, **Elmarie Dyke Open Space**. This collection of picnic tables and flowering plants honors "Mrs. Pacific Grove," one of those energetic, smart and capable women whom I always think of as simply having been born too soon. Had she started life in, say, 1956 instead of her birth year of 1896, she probably would be running a major corporation or even serving in Congress. Instead, she had to do the best she could in mid-20th century America, devoting herself to local civic affairs. She is best known for bringing back the **Feast of Lanterns**, a long-standing community tradition that had been dormant since **World War II**, running it for years with a focused-and-iron hand.

Cross Central Avenue to find the **Centrella Inn** directly across the street from Chautauqua Hall. Built in 1888 to 1889 to service the summer visitors attending the **Methodist Retreat** and **Chautauqua Assembly**, it served as a rooming house for a good portion of the 20th century. Through the decades it became a bit, shall we say, run down. In 1981, new owners came to the rescue, restoring the authentic Victorian-era styling and opening The Centrella in its current incarnation as a bed-and-breakfast inn. Today it is one of the romantic vacation venues for which Pacific Grove is famed.

From the Centrella, turn north on 16th Street, downhill toward the bay. Either side of this street is lined with **delightful Victorian cottages**, lovingly maintained by their owners. Why so small, and why such tiny lots? These houses started life as tents during the Methodist Retreat, held during the summer months in the 1870s. For $50, you could buy a 30-by-60 foot lot—just large enough for a wooden

frame and canvas tent. In the early 1900s, the seasonal tent city had transitioned into a year-'round town. Houses replaced the tents, often built directly over the canvas to provide additional insulation. A common construction style of the era was **board-and-batten**—alternating wide boards and narrow strips known as battens.

Turn right at Ocean View Boulevard, walk one block east, and then make another right onto Forest Avenue for more examples of Pacific Grove's lovely Victorian homes. I happen to be especially fond of the collection of **Pueblo-style bungalows** on either side of the foot of the street, even though their vintage is undoubtedly later than the Victorian era—1920s, I would guess. Still, they're adorable.

Cross Central Avenue to arrive at the **Pacific Grove Museum of Natural History,** taking up the entire block bordered by Forest and Grand. If by now you've guessed that this local landmark, like so many in our town, traces its roots to the Methodist Retreat, you would win the prize. The Methodists were closely entwined with the Chautauqua movement and its focus on scientific pursuits. The late Victorian era saw an upswing of interest in nature, thanks largely to the writings of **John Muir.** Those who had the

wealth and leisure time to pursue hobbies were passionate collectors of whatever struck their fancy—sea shells, fossils, bird eggs, pressed flowers, Indian arrowheads, and on and on. The timing couldn't have been better for these early Pagrovians to decide they needed a place to store and display their collections.

In 1883, the **Chautauqua Museum** opened in a small octagonal building in Jewell Park. Its first curator was a woman, **Miss E.B. Norton**. In 1902, the Pacific Improvement Company donated the land and the buildings standing on it to what was by then known as the **Pacific Grove Museum Association**. Those buildings were joined together and formed the nucleus of today's museum. An ambitious expansion project in 1983 added a large meeting hall, more exhibit space, offices, a basement for storing artifacts, and modern restroom facilities.

The city took over ownership and operation of the museum in 1916, an arrangement that remained until 2009, when the city, while retaining ownership, turned over day-to-day operation to the nonprofit **Museum Foundation of Pacific Grove**.

Today, the museum is accredited by the **American**

Alliance of Museums with permanent exhibits that include monarch butterflies, the Chinese fishing village, Native American baskets, local geology, and the birds of Monterey County. A native garden sits directly behind the building, featuring drought-resistant plants, an ethno-botanical garden focused on local native tribes, and even a fossil pit.

Whether you venture inside the museum or not, you'll certainly want to snap a photo or two at the 8,000 pound whale sculpture that rests outside. **Sandy**, as the sculpture is known, was a true labor of love for an Oakland artist, Larry Foster. In 1974, he created this life-size sculpture out of chicken wire and ferro-cement. His original intent was for Sandy to be a traveling exhibit to raise public awareness to save these giant sea mammals, and thus he designed it in sections for somewhat easier transport. Sandy made her way from Oakland to CalTech in Pasadena, and later to Santa Barbara, Boston, Philadelphia and San Francisco. When Sandy arrived in Pacific Grove in 1981, children and adults alike were enchanted. "It breathed life into the museum," said then-assistant director Paul Finnegan.

Talk began circulating around town of purchasing the sculpture. The only thing standing in the way was a price tag of $24,000. These days, you'd probably mount an online GoFundMe campaign. In the 1980s, you raised this kind of dough the old-fashioned way: pancake breakfasts, art auctions, wine tastings, and donation jars in businesses throughout the community. A clever marketing campaign allowed folks to "buy" a piece of Sandy for $3 per pound, complete with certificate of ownership. Donations poured in locally and from all over the nation. In 1983, the goal was reached and Sandy became a permanent and much-photographed part of the Pacific Grove landscape.

The Museum of Natural History is open daily from 10:00 a.m. to 5:00 p.m. Free admission for Monterey County residents, otherwise $8.95 for adults, $5.95 for youth, students and military.

From the museum, walk uphill one block on Grand Avenue to our starting point at the Holman building, completing Pacific Grove's circle of history.

JOHN STEINBECK COTTAGE

ED RICKETTS HOME

#13 STROLLING WITH STEINBECK

Today I have been thinking constantly of Pacific Grove.
—John Steinbeck, in a letter to his family in 1927

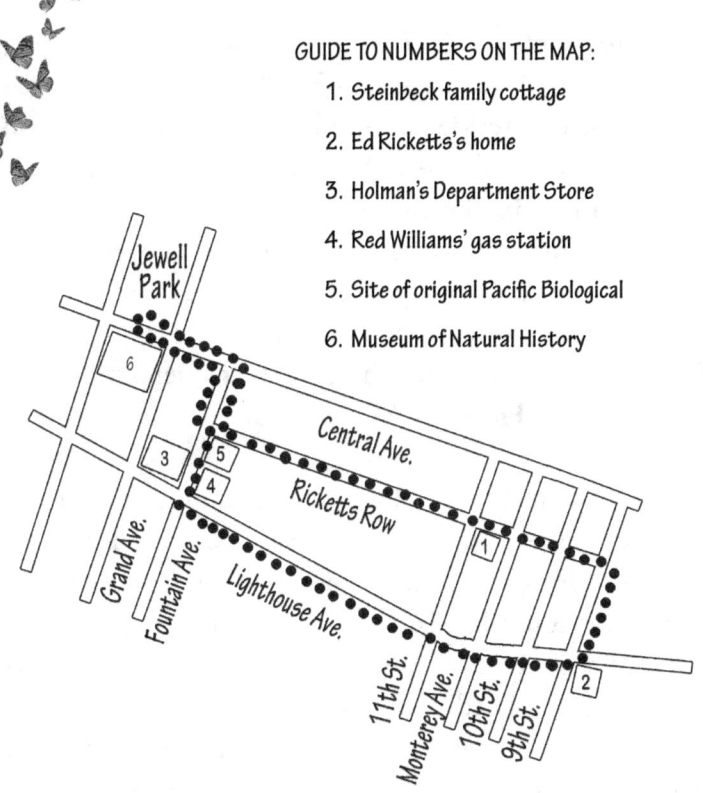

GUIDE TO NUMBERS ON THE MAP:
1. Steinbeck family cottage
2. Ed Ricketts's home
3. Holman's Department Store
4. Red Williams' gas station
5. Site of original Pacific Biological
6. Museum of Natural History

Downtown Pacific Grove and surrounding residential neighborhoods

- One mile loop/±2000 steps
- Surface: Concrete sidewalk, asphalt road, some inclines
- Public restrooms: None
- Parking: Free and unlimited on residential streets.

In Brief: *The Nobel Prize-winning author is usually associated with Salinas, but he has a strong connection with Pacific Grove, both as a resident and as a setting for his stories.*

◘ ◘ ◘

We shall start our Steinbeck stroll at the red-and-white **Steinbeck family cottage** at 147 11th Street. Please note that this is a private residence—do not disturb the occupants.

Like many well-to-do families that lived in California's inland valleys in the first decade of the 20th century, the Steinbecks of Salinas owned a seaside cottage where mother and children could escape during the hot summer months, father joining on weekends. Steinbeck and his sisters spent their childhood summers here, with frequent trips to **Lovers Point** and **Hopkins Marine Station** that developed an early interest in marine biology.

In 1930, just married to **Carol Henning** and struggling to make a career out of writing, Steinbeck received a gift of enormous importance for a young writer: his father said he and Carol could live in the cottage rent-free, *and* he contributed $25 per month toward their living expenses. With a roof over his head and at least meager sustenance on the table, Steinbeck was free to write. And write he did, producing his first major work, *Tortilla Flat*, behind these walls.

He was plugging away on *Of Mice and Men* when disaster struck. A new puppy, Toby, chewed up the one and only copy of the manuscript. An ardent dog-lover, Steinbeck took it in stride, telling his literary agent, "The poor fellow may have been acting critically."

Steinbeck was essentially a shy man who craved seclusion and anonymity. By 1936, his increasing fame made living in Pacific Grove uncomfortable. He and Carol decamped for Monte Sereno, in what is today Silicon Valley. Yet he continued to return to Pacific Grove throughout the next dozen or so years, whenever he felt the tug of fog and cool breezes, and the need to escape from marital difficulties and the demands of worldwide celebrity.

In 1949, he left California for New York with his third wife, **Elaine Scott**, and for all intents and purposes never looked back. He did make a bittersweet return to Monterey in 1960 in the trip that became *Travels with Charley* but the book makes no mention of his venturing into Pacific Grove.

Steinbeck's final journey to Pacific Grove took place after his death on December 20, 1968, at age 66. His ashes are buried in the Steinbeck plot in the **Garden of Memories in Salinas**. But before the interment took place, his widow arranged for the ashes to rest for two days in the garden in this cottage by the sea that had provided both refuge and launching pad for a young writer decades earlier.

From the Steinbeck cottage, turn east on Ricketts Row and walk three blocks. Turn right on Ninth Street, cross Lighthouse Avenue, and then head east until you reach Eighth Street. The house at the southeast corner, #331, was the one-time **home of Ed Ricketts** and his wife and children in the 1920s. Once again, a reminder that this is a private home—please be respectful!

A wife? Children? Steinbeck aficionados are to be forgiven if they express surprise that the real **Ed Ricketts** did not exactly match the hedonistic, womanizing non-conformist of *Cannery Row* and *Sweet Thursday*. Steinbeck took a great deal of literary license in his creation. Ricketts did, indeed, have a wife and three children—never mentioned in the books.

Today, we'd consider the relationship between Steinbeck and Ricketts a true "bromance," a meeting of the minds, kindred spirits. The marine biologist greatly shaped the writer's philosophy and world-view. Ricketts was the inspiration not only for the character of Doc, but also makes appearances in the guise of fictional characters in *The Grapes of Wrath, In Dubious Battle*, and *The Moon is Down*.

During Ricketts' era, traditional research in marine biology—and biology in general—was conducted by studying individual species in isolation. Decades before "ecology" became a political statement, Ricketts believed in the concept of wholeness, that one must study the individual as part of a community, that the actions of one affects all.

Turn west on Lighthouse Avenue, heading toward the downtown business district. Cross Lighthouse at Fountain Avenue to plant yourself at the northeast corner, at the site of one of the most memorable scenes of *Cannery Row*—the flagpole skater above **Holman's Department Store.**

This fanciful story starts out with fact. Store owner **W.R. Holman,** the consummate promoter, was looking for unusual ways to drum up business during the **Great Depression.** When he heard about a daredevil calling himself **"The Mysterious Mister X"** who offered to skate on a small platform situated around a flagpole at the top of the building for at least 50 hours, that seemed just the ticket.

In Steinbeck's telling of the tale, the entire town was abuzz, obsessed with just one delicate question that no one was willing to speak out loud. A Mrs. Trolat wondered about it as she left the **Scotch Bakery** (across the street at 545 Lighthouse, now a café) with a bag of sweet buns. Henri the painter sat for hours contemplating the puzzle in a chair leaned against the lattice that concealed the men's room at

Red Williams' gas station at the corner of Lighthouse and Fountain where we now stand. The service station was extensively modernized in the 1950s and in more recent decades, housed a variety of small businesses. Considered by many to be an eyesore in our beautiful historic downtown, the building was recently demolished. As of this writing the land is being developed into a combination of retail and luxury condos.

Finally a young man dared to shout out to the flagpole skater the question on everyone's mind that no one dared ask—what did he do when nature called? "I've got a can up here," came the reply.

Holman's was the place where everyone on the Monterey Peninsula shopped, and Steinbeck was no exception. During the Pacific Grove years when money was tight, he wrote his manuscripts in green ink purchased at Holman's. Green ink sold for two bottles for a nickel, whereas one bottle of blue ink would have cost him a dime. One particular penurious Thanksgiving, Steinbeck found a discarded *papier-mâché* turkey behind the store, took it home and used it to disguise the real Thanksgiving feast— a pile of cheap hamburgers.

Walk down the right side of Fountain Avenue to #165, where a plaque marks the 1923 location of **Ed Ricketts' first lab**, before he moved **Pacific Biological** to its more famous location on **Cannery Row** in 1928. Placed by the Heritage Society and the Museum of Natural History, the plaque notes, "Ricketts' studies of intertidal marine life became benchmarks in ecological science."

Look upward at the street sign at the alley that runs just behind the paint store. **Ricketts Row** was dedicated July 14, 1994, replacing the earlier name of High Street. This alley connects two significant Steinbeck sites in Pacific Grove, the first location of Pacific Biological and the Steinbeck family cottage.

Continue downhill on Fountain, turn left on Central and walk one block west to the **Pacific Grove Museum of Natural History**. Described in detail in walk #12-Historic Downtown, the museum's exhibits includes a giant squid preserved in formaldehyde, donated by Ed Ricketts.

Cross Central Avenue to **Jewell Park**, site of "The Great Roque War" in Chapter 8 of *Sweet Thursday*. Steinbeck delighted in poking gentle fun at the quirky ways of his second hometown, still feeling the influence of the straitlaced Methodists some 50 years after their arrival. After listing the various amusements and sins banned in Pacific Grove, he notes the one, overarching, unwritten rule: "Hijinks are or is forbidden."

Like the Holman's flagpole skater, the roque war had some basis in fact. Roque is a game similar to croquet, but played on a concrete court and with shorter mallets, and saw its greatest popularity at the turn of the 20th century. For many years, Jewell Park featured a roque court on the northeast corner, where the gazebo now stands.

In 1933, one of those civic imbroglios that Pacific Grove seems to attract like a magnet broke out when word spread that the roque court was going to be removed in order to widen Central Avenue. The debate got so heated that the city council members threw up their hands in defeat, sending it to the voters for a decision. By an overwhelming margin, the citizens sided with the roque court, moving it farther into the park to make way for the road improvement project. How long it remained seems lost to history, though the roque court is obviously gone now.

In Steinbeck's telling of the tale, the "Great Roque War"

escalated to family feuds, mallet attacks and burnings in effigy. At the end, though, he does admit that he might have made up the whole story, "but a thing isn't necessarily a lie even if it didn't necessarily happen."

I cannot help but wonder what fun Steinbeck would have with the current dust-up in our town over pickleball. Surely a sequel would be in the works—"The Great Pickleball War" anyone?

From Jewell Park, walk back to the site of Ricketts' first lab on Fountain Avenue and then make your way east on Ricketts Row until you arrive on 11th Street and the start of this tour.

Other Steinbeck sites in Pacific Grove accessible by bicycle or automobile:

The Great Tidepool: Just north of the intersection of Lighthouse Avenue and Ocean View Boulevard. Described in detail in Walk #3 – Asilomar Coast Trail.

425 Eardley Avenue: Steinbeck lived in this cottage briefly in 1941 during the break-up with his marriage to Carol and his affair with the woman who would become the second Mrs. Steinbeck, **Gwyn Conger.** Yet another reminder that this is a private home; please respect the privacy of the current occupants.

Esther Steinbeck Rodgers Home: Now part of the Asilomar Conference Grounds and described in more detail in Walk #6. Steinbeck's sister and her husband, **Carroll Rodgers,** lived here from the 1930s to the 1950s.

Elizabeth Hamilton's Cottage: This small private residence at 222 Central Avenue was the home of Steinbeck's maternal grandmother, **Elizabeth Hamilton,** from 1915 to 1918. Though the famous author never actually lived here, that didn't stop a Steinbeck fan from turning it into a quirky little homegrown museum in the 1990s. Those residing in or visiting Pacific Grove in the early years of the 21st century will well remember the larger-than-life gold-painted statue of the author in the front yard, greeting all who passed by on Central Avenue. New owners have since remodeled the home and removed the statue. It found a new home with artist Snick Farkas, who poked fun at the **"Colossus of Gold"** in cartoons in the local newspaper.

COURTESY SNICK FARKAS

#14 CANDY CANE LANE

Walking in a winter wonderland...
—Felix Bernard and Richard B. Smith, 1934

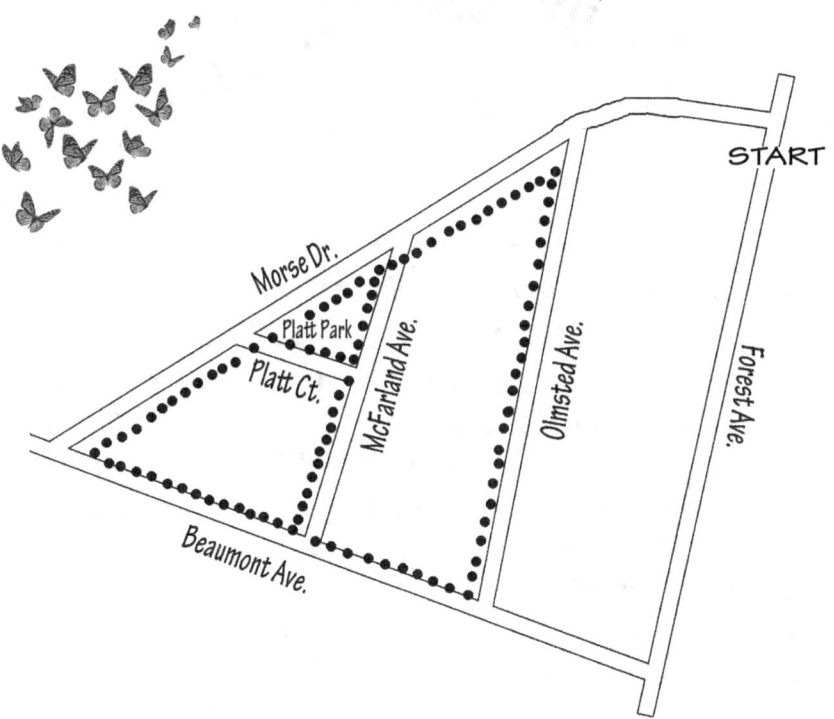

Neighborhood bounded by Morse Drive and Beaumont Avenue off of Forest Avenue

- At most, a one mile loop/±2000 steps
- Surface: Concrete sidewalk and asphalt road
- Public restrooms: None
- Parking: Free on residential streets. Overflow parking available at Pacific Grove's nearby middle and high schools.

In Brief: *Our holiday bonus, a stroll through Pacific Grove's traditional Christmas-themed neighborhood, usually open the first Saturday in December and running through New Year's Eve.*

City maps from the 1930s give this neighborhood the name of **Country Club Heights,** but today everyone knows it as Candy Cane Lane—so much so that some visitors are puzzled when they cannot find a street with that actual name on their GPS. Homes began appearing on the already-laid out streets before **World War II,** but most arrived post-war. By the mid-1950s, the area was already getting a reputation as a place where the residents went all-out when it came to decorating their homes for Christmas.

Today the neighborhood consists of 75 houses. Nearly all the residents get into the holiday spirit by decorating their homes and donating money for upkeep of the common area displays. No one has ever made an official count, but it's safe to say annual visitors number in the thousands. They come from all over the Monterey Peninsula to soak in the spirit of the most Christmassy neighborhood for miles around. Most stay in their cars, creating a glacial, bumper-to-bumper scenario of near gridlock as the days inch towards the 25th.

◘ ◘ ◘

But this is a walking book, so that is what we shall do, ditching the car and enjoying Candy Cane Lane on foot. Dress warmly—sure, this is California, but it is December—and watch out for all those cars! You can be certain the drivers are easily distracted by the lighted displays and may not be focused on pedestrians.

The focal point for all this holly-jolly spirit is **Platt Park**, a three-tenths of an acre triangular-shaped plot of land bordered by Morse Drive, McFarland Avenue and Platt Court. For those with small children in tow, a stroll around the park may be enough. Named for **Dr. Julia Platt**, Pacific Grove's first female mayor and an early environmental activist, during the holiday season it becomes a true winter wonderland. Moving displays include a Ferris wheel, a swinging Santa, and miniature train. Then there are the painted plywood cutouts of cartoon characters. Dozens and dozens of them: Snoopy, Buzz Lightyear, the Disney princesses. Whoever is hot with the kiddie set during a given year.

Occasionally someone will ask what cartoon characters like SpongeBob SquarePants have to do with "the reason for the season." The answer: the kids love them, and that's what Candy Cane Lane is all about. Delighting the children.

The in-motion displays are fenced off with netting, preventing kids from actually running in and around them. This is due to safety concerns, electricity and moving parts usually not a good combination with tiny tots. Outside the fenced area the kids are welcome to explore a gingerbread house, while a sleigh provides the perfect setting for a family photograph.

To admire the decorated homes, from Platt Park head

in a northeast direction on Morse Drive. Turn left at Beaumont, and make another left on McFarland. The displays on the individual homes may vary from year to year, depending on who lives there and how ambitious they feel. An Elvis-themed house, complete with "Blue Christmas," has been a long-time fixture. During recent years, some residents have taken to selling hot chocolate from their doorsteps. Teens from local school bands have been known to offer live entertainment. Much like opening a wrapped Christmas gift, you never quite know for sure what you'll get when you visit Candy Cane Lane.

For decades one of the most talked-about and photographed displays graced a home at the corner of Beaumont and McFarland. This 15-foot nutcracker (or is it a toy soldier?) has now joined the rest of the displays at Platt Park. With its moving arms and jaw and lighted eyes, the thing is either festive, campy, or downright creepy depending on your point of view. I've heard various origin stories, either as a giant fireman in front of the P.G. Fire Department, or as a robotic greeter for a Boy Scout jamboree at the Monterey fairgrounds back in the 1960s. Since the creator, the late Howard Cowen, was both a volunteer fireman and a Scoutmaster (as well as one of the guiding forces behind Candy Cane Lane), either story could hold a grain of truth. And just for the record, Mr. Cowen referred to the metal giant as **"Pierre the Nut Cracker."**

You may either return to Platt Park on McFarland, or if you're feeling ambitious, continue west on Beaumont, make a left on Olmstead, and another left on Morse to return to the park.

Candy Cane Lane is also the go-to place for trick-or-treating on the Monterey Peninsula, with one homeowner estimating she serves around 1,500 "customers" every Halloween. It's a safe, kid-friendly neighborhood where most homeowners welcome the visits by the pint-sized ghosts and goblins.

Perhaps that's the real magic of this otherwise nondescript collection of mid-century modern tract homes on the southern edge of town. It's a place where the residents know each other, watch out for each other, and band together once a year for no other purpose than to sprinkle a little joy into the lives of children of all ages. The very essence of the Christmas spirit

New releases for 2021
PACIFIC GROVE BOOKS

Here for the Present – Live, from the Poet's Perch
Barbara Mossberg, PhD, Illustrated by Sophia Mossberg
ISBN 978-1-953120-14-4

Tea Table
Chef Karen Anne Murray's
Inspiring Teatime Creations from Pacific Grove, CA
ISBN 978-1-953120-25-0

W. R. Holman Autobiography
W.R. Holman, Annotated by Heather Lazare
ISBN 978-1-953120-15-1

A Piney Paradise by Monterey Bay
The Early History of Pacific Grove
Lucy Neely McLane, Fifth Edition by Patricia Hamilton
ISBN 978-1-953120-19-9

Minnow – Tales of the Lighthouse
A Work of Fact-based Fiction by Fred Sammis
ISBN 978-1-953120-11-3

All PacificGr ove Books are available from:
On-line vendors, pacificgr ovebooks.com,
and at the Bookworks in downtown PG.

*A donation is made to the
Friends of the Pacific Grove Library
for every book sold.*

PACIFIC GROVE BOOKS
Pacific Grove, California

Bringing Our Community Together – Through the Power of Story